7 tools for coping with stress and uncertainty

Stillness
in the
Storm

Jan Alcoe and Dr Sarah Eagger

The Janki Foundation for Spirituality in Healthcare
Email: info@jankifoundation.org
Web: www.jankifoundation.org

Cover and interior design: Phil Morash
Illustrations: Tanya John (tanyasuzannejohn@gmail.com)
Printed by: Ashford Press
Audio recordings: see end of book
An e book of this publication is also available
https://www.jankifoundation.org/stillness-in-the-storm/

DISCLAIMER: Important note for the reader
The suggestions, exercises and audio recordings presented in this book are not intended as a substitute for a consultation with, or advice from, qualified medical or psychotherapeutic professionals. The author and publishers cannot be held responsible for any loss, claim or damage arising from the use or misuse of materials in the book, or the failure to take medical advice.

Dedication

This book is dedicated to our two dear friends who both passed way in the Spring of 2020:

Dadi Janki

Our founding president of the Janki Foundation for Spiritual Healthcare who was a constant source of compassion, inspiration and encouragement.

Dr Craig Brown

Our scientific and medical advisor and former trustee who was a great supporter, innovator and contributor to the work of the Janki Foundation.

Acknowledgements

Arnold Desser and Peter Dale for feedback on the draft of the book. Dr Rachna Chowla, Dr Julia Ronder and Suman Kalra for reading the manuscript and for their support. Suman Kalra for writing some of the positive affirmations. Tanya John for illustrations, Michael Benge for copy editing, Dan Betts for technical audio assistance and Steph Jury for help with cover design.

This book draws upon many skills and approaches we have learnt through our years of training and clinical work. We are extremely grateful for all the inspirations and ideas which have informed us on the journey of writing this book. In particular, we extend gratitude to the *Values in Healthcare programme* (Janki Foundation, 2004), *Gilbert's Compassionate Mind* model (Constable, 2009), and Neff and Germer's *Mindful Self-Compassion Course* (Guilford Press, 2013), which informed the content of Chapter 3 in particular.

For acknowledgements relating to particular practices and the audio recordings, please see the back of the book.

Authors

Jan Alcoe (BSSc PsychHons, DHypPsych(UK)) is publishing and training adviser to the Janki Foundation and has a background in writing and publishing in health and social care. She is trained in clinical hypnotherapy and has written two previous Janki Foundation self-help guides based on her professional experience and from coping with personal, serious illness. She co-edited the self-development programme *Values in Healthcare: a spiritual approach* for the Janki Foundation. Jan has retained a lifelong interest in positive psychology, the power of the mind-body connection and spirituality in healing, and was a past vice-chair of the British Holistic Medical Association.

Dr Sarah Eagger (MB,BS, FRCPsych) is Chair of the Janki Foundation. She worked for 30 years in the NHS as a consultant psychiatrist and honorary senior clinical lecturer in the department of Psychological Medicine, Imperial College, London, and also worked in private practice for 15 years. Sarah is executive committee member of the World Psychiatric Association, Section on Religion, Spirituality and Psychiatry and past chair of the Spirituality Special Interest Group of the Royal College of Psychiatrists, the National Spirituality and Mental Health Forum and the British Holistic Medical Association. As a practitioner of raja yoga meditation for over 40 years and a certified Mindful Self-Compassion teacher, she is an advocate of a values-based approach to healthcare – one that embraces peace, love, positivity and compassion for the benefit of oneself and others.

Contents

Foreword   **6**

Preface   **7**

Introduction   **9**

Why this guide?   10
Fear and doing versus calm   11
Returning to wholeness: our spiritual nature   13
What this self-help guide offers   14
Who is this guide for?   16
How to use this guide   17
Before you begin, relax!   18

Chapter 1: Creating Inner Safety   **19**

Chapter 2: Being Present   **31**

Chapter 3: Loving Myself   **43**

Chapter 4: Stepping Back and Accepting   **55**

Chapter 5: Empowering Myself   **67**

Chapter 6: Connecting   **83**

Chapter 7: Discovering Inner Peace and Wholeness   **93**

Chapter 8: Resilience Beyond the Storm   **105**

Audio commentaries

You can access the 20 audio commentaries referred to
in this book by going to:
https://www.jankifoundation.org/stillness-in-the-storm-audios/

Foreword

I would like to thank Jan Alcoe and Dr Sarah Eagger for writing this book. At this time of multiple 'storms', when humanity seems to be lurching from one crisis to another, even deeper one, it offers simple, spiritual self-care practices that can help us all return to our natural state of calm.

I have known Sarah most of my life and have seen how she has devoted her life to serving humanity. At the same time, I have seen how she has given attention to her own personal spiritual journey, so as to nurture and empower herself in her work supporting others. I have known Jan, too, for many years and what has struck me most is her willingness, as a medical editor, to go into the depth of values in healthcare from a spiritual perspective. I have seen Jan go through a period of critical illness and come out the other side with a lot of lightness, experience and wisdom. She has used spiritual tools in her own life to keep herself moving forward,

The unimagined changes we are witnessing in the world and experiencing in our lives are having a huge impact on the well-being, sense of identity and feelings of connectedness and belonging of individuals and communities worldwide. At such times, when our routines, choices and pastimes are no longer possible or curtailed, it is understandable that we can feel we are no longer in control, anxious and lost. Yet it is often precisely when external supports are taken away from us that we can see and understand more clearly and deeply what is going on inside – our thoughts and feelings – and start to know and take care of ourselves better. The more we connect and identify with that inner self with its eternal, innate qualities of peace, love, wisdom and joy, the better we equip ourselves to respond, adjust and contribute to the situations we face calmly and constructively.

It's great and so timely to have a book like this and I know that these 7 spiritual tools, if applied in life, will definitely bring a lot of benefit.

Sister Jayanti
European Director of Brahma Kumaris

Preface

At the time of writing this self-help guide, we find ourselves in the midst of a coronavirus pandemic which has plunged us into a world of uncertainty and created extreme levels of personal, social and economic disruption. Never before have we been asked to isolate ourselves physically from other human beings, just when we yearn to reach out and embrace each other to show our mutual love and support. Sadly, it is the most vulnerable who will suffer the worst, and many of us will be forced to watch their distress from a distance, while being powerless to stand alongside them in physical form. Many will become physically sick but others will become mentally unwell, cast adrift in a lonely, fearful place. Following on the heels of some major climate catastrophes that have uprooted whole populations, and set alongside continuing wars that destroy lives and homes and cause huge numbers of refugees to search for safety, it is indeed a time that most of us have never seen in our memory. It is as if the world has been enveloped in a major storm, bringing darkness, uncertainty and confusion all around. How can we develop the inner resilience we will need to weather the storm and to emerge stronger and more connected?

This book provides some simple tools for dealing with our own fears and creating a stable, inner core from which we can move away from emotional distress and be of service to ourselves, our families and communities. This is particularly important when the world around us seems out of control. However bad a storm, we know that the sun continues to shine somewhere beyond. There may also be silver linings. Already there are signs that worldwide crises prompt human responses of love and support for others and even heroic sacrifice, as we come to realise our interconnectedness. Even while the coronavirus storm rages around us, by recovering our sense of calm, we can find our way back to the light, overcome our anxiety and begin to act more resourcefully. All storms pass eventually, and hopefully we will emerge with a sense of how to live more peacefully and authentically in full recognition of our inter-dependence.

We offer you a simple guide for self-help at this time. It might also be called a self-discovery guide, as some of the chapters delve into deeper philosophical and psychological aspects of resilience which we hope can inspire reflection and further study. The book does not need to be studied or read from cover to cover. The practices and recordings it contains can be selected at random according to your current needs. No one practice takes very long and so you can pick them up when you have just a minute or two and want to foster a sense of calm. However, the more you practise and listen, the more readily you will restore your equilibrium when the winds blow and you find yourself knocked off course. We wish you well.

Jan Alcoe and Sarah Eagger

NB If you are coping with physical illness, or want to use the time you may have to develop your overall well-being, there are two companion self-help books with recordings available from the Janki Foundation (see below). These are:

Lifting Your Spirits: seven tools for coping with illness by Jan Alcoe
www.jankifoundation.org/lifting-your-spirits/

Heart of Well-being: seven tools for surviving and thriving by Jan Alcoe
www.jankifoundation/the-heart-of-well-being/

Additionally, Happidote is an app for healthcare professionals to access simple guided meditations to soothe the stress of work www. jankifoundation.org/happidote

About the Janki Foundation for Spirituality in Healthcare

The Janki Foundation is a UK charity promoting the integration of spirituality into healthcare. The Foundation acknowledges the central role of positive thoughts and feelings, compassion and kindness in maintaining well-being and preventing illness. Through publications, experiential learning, talks, and networking, the Foundation provides opportunities to further such approaches among individuals and professionals. It also gives regular financial support to a hospital in Rajasthan, India, that has pioneered a healthcare model combining modern medical technology with spirituality and complementary medicine.

www.jankifoundation.org

The Foundation's activities are free of charge and managed wholly by volunteers. Contributions to further the Foundation's work are most welcome. Donations support our educational activities and the work of the Global Hospital and Research Centre in Mt Abu, India. This is an area where poverty is high and free treatment is provided to a large number of patients.

https://www.jankifoundation.org/donate/

Introduction

Why this guide?

This self-help guide is for all of us who wish to live a fulfilling and contented life in an uncertain world. The tools it offers help us to weather the storms around us by digging inner foundations of calm. In that way, however strongly the weather rages, we can stand firm and act resourcefully, staying true to ourselves, rather than being blown around in a maelstrom of fear. We know that eventually the bad weather will pass, but discovering calm within the storm will help us to keep the sun in our sights in everything we think and do.

We live in an uncertain world that is changing and unstable in almost every dimension – political, social, climatic, economic – relayed to us from across the globe in a continuous flow via social media and TV. Graphic images of chaos and human suffering can lead us to experience general anxiety, fear, anger or even vicarious trauma. Most of us exist in a society characterised by over-stimulation, high expectations and too much choice about what we do and have, all of which can fuel our anxiety and impair our decision-making. At a family level, some of us may have grown up in difficult or abusive circumstances that have damaged our self-confidence and capacity to claim our right to a healthy and fulfilling life. We may feel so small, insignificant or even ashamed that we become prey to those who would use us for their own ends. Individual events – an accident, death of loved ones, serious illness, bullying and other psychological and physical events – can lead to many forms of emotional distress. It is not surprising that our modern societies experience rising levels of depression and other mental health problems in both adults and children.

Chronic anxiety and the inability to calm the mind and spirit can lead to physical ill health, emotional numbing, a more negative view of the world and loss of enjoyment of life. We may withdraw from others, leading to fractured relationships, and an inability to empathise with the plight of others. We lose the sense of who we really are and what is important as our sense of self shrinks or even fragments. In an effort to feel safer and back in control, we can unconsciously try to meet our needs in ways that cause further emotional suffering for ourselves and others, for example turning to over-eating, addictive substances or self-harm. There is a tendency for us to dwell on the many 'bad' things that happen or have happened, while a whole host of positive and kind acts go unnoticed. This fuels emotions of anger and fear and impairs our capacity to see life events from a more helpful and hopeful perspective. How can we recover our more spiritual and whole selves, capable of compassion for ourselves and others, and be able to draw on our immense inner resources to cope with what is going on around us?

Fear and doing versus calm

The key to beginning this inner journey is to access the part of the nervous system that can lead us back to calm. The more primitive part of our brain evolved to save us from danger and is characterised by an automatic and immediate 'fight or flight' response when we perceive a threat. When faced with a wild animal, a speeding car or an aggressive intruder, this kick-starts a whole host of physiological changes in our bodies to enable us to escape or stand our ground and fight. Our bodies are flooded with stress hormones, such as adrenalin, that raise our heart rates and blood pressure, diverting blood flow into the big muscles and away from unnecessary functions like digestion, or even thinking, so that we can save ourselves in the moment. It is only when the threat has passed that we find ourselves sweating, shaking and breathless, but hopefully out of danger. It can take some time for us to calm down from such an extreme physical and emotional reaction. While the rapid *threat/defence* response is vital to our survival at times, it can be also triggered by strong emotions like anger, disgust or fear when we remember past difficulties and trauma, watch upsetting scenes on a screen, or conjure up difficult thoughts about what might happen in the future. This part of our brain is unable to distinguish reality from our vivid imaginations and so our survival system can come into play before we have time to consider or think about what is really happening.

Long-term, the constant firing of the threat/defence response, and the outpouring of stress hormones that accompany it, can lead to a whole host of physical and mental health problems, from high blood pressure, insomnia and impaired immune response to depression and chronic anxiety. Long-term stress, or even a tendency to self-criticism, can provoke similar reactions, with all its inherent dangers for our well-being. Being in this state of heightened fear or stress impairs and narrows our thinking so that we are unable to keep things in any helpful perspective.

Another mind/body system we use is the active or *'doing'* system. This mainly uses dopamine, a chemical released by nerve cells to send signals to other nerve cells, to get things done. However, it is linked to our motivational drive for and experience of pleasure, and can be highly addictive. It can lead us to check our e-mails or social media messages obsessively, or at worst, to indulge in risky or dangerous behaviours like gambling or substance mis-use. It can make it hard for us to stop 'doing' and slow down, leading to burnout or exhaustion.

We cannot help but react emotionally when we are under threat, or sometimes to feel driven to keep on working, even though we should rest. However, we can learn to recover quickly by activating another, *soothing* pathway of the nervous system. This part calms and relaxes us physically and mentally, restoring vital functions for physical health and helping us to stay hopeful and resourceful in times of uncertainty and challenge. It can be activated by meditation, slow breathing, loving and kind thoughts, and other practices that are included in this book. It develops from the bonding between mother and child, making us feel safe, secure and connected. When we are able to feel safe and calm despite the storm, we can think and act in ways that are most beneficial for ourselves and for others around us.

While all three of the systems briefly described above have a function in our lives, for most of us, these are out of balance and we may find that most of our day is activated by the threat/defence system or the doing system. This book is designed to bring the soothing system more into play and to promote recovery and calm.

Returning to wholeness: our spiritual nature

As human beings we have physical, mental and emotional aspects to our lives and well-being. Additionally, there is a spiritual dimension to our existence. Whether or not we believe in a divine presence or have a religious practice, there is an inner core to our being that gives us our unique identity and sense of wholeness. We may tap into it when we contemplate the wonder of nature or become absorbed in a creative activity. We may become aware that there is an essence within that transcends all the roles we play in life and our outer identity, providing us with a deep experience of inner strength, integrity and peace. It also connects to something beyond ourselves, whether this is a community, the natural world, universal energy or the divine, and we feel part of a bigger whole.

At times of great uncertainty and change, this sense of spiritual wholeness can be a vital support, even when we are isolated from others. We can reframe the challenge we face as an opportunity to learn, grow and rediscover who we really are. It can move us away from trying to fill the emotional gaps by looking to others or relying on negative or harmful behaviours. We can, instead, focus on small, positive practices that utilise and build on our strengths and values. We become less self-centred and more aware of our interconnectedness, moving away from the 'us' and 'them' thinking that we can fall into as a result of our experience of fear.

What this self-help guide offers

There are many self-help guides that focus on anxiety and offer advice and practices often based on one particular therapeutic model or psychological approach. This guide draws from many of the ideas and techniques that are used to treat anxiety and distress, but approaches them from the perspective of spiritual well-being. The emphasis is on using spiritual tools to recover our identity of wholeness and connection, to make sense of personal challenges, and to maintain a stable core of calm and resourcefulness within.

The 7 Spiritual Tools

Each tool in this book reminds us of our essence, our spiritual self that connects us to a stable core within and a rediscovery of calm.

1. Creating inner safety

Creating a special place of safety within our minds by using our mental power to visualise, helps us to calm right down and to soothe our minds and senses.

2. Being present

Coming fully into the present moment through mindfulness practice moves us away from fearful thoughts about the future and hands back a sense of control in chaotic times. Most importantly, it enables us to come to terms with things as they are.

3. Loving myself
Learning self-compassion is an important step towards healing the distress of past events, accepting myself as I am, and developing compassion for others.

4. Stepping back and accepting
Learning how to stand back from the drama of life and witness our own thoughts and actions puts difficult events into perspective and frees us to respond resourcefully, rather than from a place of fear or panic.

5. Empowering myself
Expressing who we truly are and forgiving ourselves and others gives us the power of agency so that we can begin to act with hope, purpose and determination.

6. Connecting
Connecting deep within and beyond ourselves helps us to identify our inner and external resources that we can draw upon in difficult times.

7. Discovering inner peace and wholeness
Through meditation practice, we can discover a sense of internal peace and wholeness to quieten any sense of turmoil on the inside.

Even practising with one of these tools for just a minute or two, it is possible to recover calm. That sense of calm provides a pathway to regaining your inner wisdom and resilience. Resilience is a concept we explore in the final chapter 'Resilience Beyond the Storm'.

Who is this guide for?

This guide is for you if you recognise the need for calming the mind and are interested in a spiritual approach, and those:

- who wish to stay on top of stress, prevent unhelpful anxiety and build or maintain a sense of calm and resourcefulness in their lives
- experiencing mild anxiety or worry who would wish to adopt helpful practices in everyday life
- facing particular challenges who want to maintain a resourceful state of mind and spirit
- recovering from more significant anxiety problems and trauma following professional intervention.

What this guide isn't – a warning note about when to seek professional help

This guide is not intended to replace seeking medical or professional help for significant mental or emotional problems, for example if you are experiencing any of the following:

- high levels of general anxiety or anger, phobias or recurring panic attacks
- significant trauma with difficulty in everyday living, sleep disturbance or flashbacks
- substance misuse, obsessive or self-harming behaviours
- symptoms of depression such as loss of motivation, loss of appetite, changes in sleeping habits, persistent negative thinking
- undiagnosed pain, physical symptoms or persistent sleep problems
- social isolation due to severe lack of confidence or self-esteem.

How to use this guide

The main part of this book contains chapters exploring each of the 7 spiritual tools. Each chapter includes the following elements:

- a brief description of the particular challenges the tool addresses and why it is so helpful in coping with fear and uncertainty
- reflections on using the tool from individuals affected by anxiety and trauma
- suggested ways of practising the tool, with clear guidance
- rescue remedies – these are quick ways to recover a sense of calm in difficult situations
- links to audio commentaries of between 4 and 30 minutes to help you experience the essence of each tool
- resourceful, calming affirmations you can say to yourself as you go through your day.

Note about using the audio commentaries

You can access the 20 audio commentaries referred to in this book by going to:
https://www.jankifoundation.org/stillness-in-the-storm-audios/

Before you listen to any of the 20 audio commentaries contained within this book, make sure you are comfortably settled in a place where you will not be disturbed for the duration of the recording. Do not listen while you are driving or need to concentrate.

You can dip into any chapter and try any tool or practice in any order. However, if you are in a crisis or find yourself beset with anxiety, the first step is to create a sense of safety. We would suggest you turn to **Chapter 1. Creating Inner Safety** and use some of the practices you can find there, including the relaxing breath, creating a safe space, self-soothing and the quick rescue remedies (pp23 – 28).

Additionally, you can practise mindful breathing in **Chapter 2. Being Present**, or use the relaxation audio recordings below.

Before you begin, relax!

Learning to relax when you are experiencing emotional distress in the present, or trying to come to terms with traumatic events from the past, can seem almost impossible. However, activating the soothing part of the nervous system described on p12 provides a pathway to your recovery. The following audio links are offered as a way of calming the breath and relaxing the body, so that you can gain full benefit from the rest of the guide. Be easy on yourself and follow the relaxation commentaries for as long as it feels comfortable. Even a few minutes of these practices will have a positive impact on how you feel and think.

 1. **Relaxing Breath (4.40 mins)**

 2. **Breathe and Relax (5.26 mins)**

Chapter 1: Creating Inner Safety

When I go to a safe space within my mind,
I recover a sense of calm and can soothe myself

One of our most basic human needs is to feel safe. When we feel threatened by real or imaginary events, our fight-flight response (described on page 11) is triggered to mobilise us to escape or fight the danger. This survival response, although useful in times of real danger, can become part of our pattern of responding and eventually can impair our well-being. When we continue to feel under threat, even when that threat has passed, we need to know how to get back to feeling safe again. It is only when we rediscover an inner sense of safety that we can begin our journey towards wholeness.

When we are stressed, we sometimes find ourselves using our powerful imaginations to conjure up potential disaster scenarios that maintain our feelings of unease or fright. The signals arriving through our senses – sounds, sights, smells, tastes and textures – can also remind us of feeling unsafe and even take us straight back to a past event that was shocking or distressing for us. Even pleasant or neutral sensations can get associated with the memories of the event we 'lay down' in the brain, so that when we hear a particular sound, or smell a particular smell, or see a particular colour, we re-experience the distress we felt at the time. This is a characteristic of 'flashbacks', post-traumatic stress and phobias. Sometimes our senses get assaulted by things that are too much to handle, for example when we may see disturbing sights in the street or on TV, we hear loud or upsetting noises or are exposed to toxic or nauseating smells.

Creating a safe space

With this first tool we can practise using our imagination and our senses in a different, more helpful way by creating a safe inner space within our minds. We can visualise somewhere that feels protected and soothing, perhaps somewhere we have been in the past, or a place that just arises in our imagination. It could be somewhere outside or inside, a space with pleasing light, colours, sounds, textures and scents. Tapping in to all the sensations of this place as we develop it in our minds – what we can see, hear, feel, smell, touch – helps us to feel safer and regain a state of calm. Even if we can't 'see pictures' of such a place, we can just get a sense of what it is like, and we can come back to it again and again when we feel stressed, afraid or anxious. Guidelines for creating a safe space are included in the 'Now Practise' section below.

> *My home was caught in spreading wild fires and was badly damaged, I found myself looking around me all the time for signs that something bad was about to happen. I felt jittery and unsafe. I worried that the fires would come again and imagined some terrible scenes. I started to practise going to a special place of safety in my mind, especially when I felt stressed or had something challenging coming up. I discovered that I could calm down quicker after any upsets and even began to get a new perspective on what had happened to me. Just being in the wrong place at the wrong time didn't mean that bad things were going to keep happening to me in the future.*

We can use our internal safe space not just to recapture a sense of calm, but in a way that gives us back a sense of control over how we react to the challenges around us. We can go into it to stay present to what is happening (see **Chapter 2**), prepare for a potentially stressful encounter or event, and cultivate our self-compassion (see **Chapter 3**). We can step back from habitual patterns (see **Chapter 4**) and practise new behaviours, visualising ourselves coping well or responding positively or calmly in the face of difficulty. We can empower ourselves, forgive, express gratitude, or create new hope (see **Chapter 5**), reducing our sense of powerlessness, fear and suffering. We can evaluate and change unhealthy beliefs and actions, and re-connect with our strengths and values (see **Chapter 6**) and discover our inner core of peace and wisdom (see **Chapter 7**).

Overall, cultivating an inner sanctuary can give ourselves a valuable opportunity to build our self-confidence and resilience (see **Chapter 8**).

Self-soothing

Having created a safe space, we can identify and use real or imagined objects and sensations to soothe our senses and help us feel calm and safe. This is called 'self-soothing'. Sometimes experiencing distress can prompt us into self-soothing that is harmful, in an effort to meet our emotional needs (see **Chapter 6**). This may include over-eating, bingeing on harmful substances, cutting the skin, compulsive gambling or high-risk sexual activity. By creating a safe space and using self-soothing in a positive way, we can begin to associate new, pleasant sensations with relaxation, safety and calm. Pleasing sounds and vibrations, colours, scents, scenes and textures can be 'felt' by our bodies as well as our minds, and can help to induce calming.

> ' *When I get tense and angry remembering what happened to me, I sometimes set aside some time to make bread. I love the feel of sifting the flour and watching it cloud up from the bowl. I really get stuck into kneading the dough and focusing on its soft, stretchy silkiness under my hands. Once in the oven, I watch though the door as it rises and turns a lovely golden brown on top, inhaling the wonderful smell that fills the kitchen. Best of all is the crunchy sound of cutting a first slice, watching the butter melt slightly on the warm crumb, and sinking my teeth into total delight! It makes me feel soothed and connected back to good things in life.'*

> *When I was going through cancer treatment, I spent a lot of time on my own at home and sometimes felt stressed and down with the uncertainty of my future. I collected some special, soothing things in a lovely box that I had kept from a previous birthday. There was a photo of a beautiful beach I had visited, some dried petals from my daughter's wedding, my favourite perfume, a small, soft toy that I had kept from my children's baby days, a card with some kind words from a friend, a small bell from Thailand that made a lovely sound. I added to my special box throughout my treatment and when I felt frightened or was in pain, just opening it and catching the scent made me feel soothed. By holding and focusing on the things inside, it helped me to remember the positive things in my life and how I was much more than just my illness.*

Learning to establish a safe inner space and to self-soothe helps us to 'switch off' the threat/defence part of the nervous system and 'switch on' the soothing part described on pp11 –13. The more we can do this, the more we begin to recover on all levels – physical, mental, emotional and spiritual – and start to see our lives and what is happening in more hopeful ways. Our inner refuge is fully portable, so we can take it with us wherever we go and into whatever situations we may find ourselves.

Now practise

My safe space

A first step to feeling safer is to visualise a 'safe space' in your mind. You can only do this when you are feeling relaxed, so use the **1.**

Relaxing Breath or **2. Breathe and Relax** audio recordings in the Introduction (p18) before you begin.

You are going to visualise a space of safety just for you. Don't worry if you can't see this place as some sort of picture in your mind. Some of us are not so visual, but may have a stronger sense of hearing or smell or touch. Just get the sense of being in the place in whatever way feels easy and natural for you.

- Spend a few minutes relaxing with slow, deep breathing and close your eyes if it feels comfortable to do so. If not, keep your eyes relaxed and softly focused ahead.
- Remember a time when you were in a place that felt safe, comfortable and completely relaxing, or imagine what such a place might be for you. It could be outside – a holiday beach, a meadow full of summer flowers; or inside – a cosy room with a crackling fire, a sanctuary or place of worship. It could be something less well defined – perhaps just a shape, textures or colours.
- Now imagine entering that place through a door or gate, closing it behind you.
- What is your place like? Take some time to look, hear, smell and feel this place in whatever ways you find easiest.
- As you practise conjuring up this space in your mind, over time you can add more and more detail – the quality of light, colours, sounds, textures and objects that add to your sense of calm and well-being.
- Find a place to rest in this space – perhaps a beautiful chair or lounger.
- As you relax in this space in your mind, know that you are completely safe and that you can visit here whenever you need, staying as long as you wish.
- Know that only you can come into this special place, unless you invite another. If you need to make it feel extra safe, throw some kind of impermeable barrier around it. This could be a high,

unscalable wall or an energy force field to keep all unwanted people and things out.

- As you relax in this space, experience what it feels like to grow a little calmer.
- When you are ready to leave your safe space, face the door or gate that you entered through. Imagine yourself opening it, stepping through and closing it behind you.
- Take a few deep breaths, look around you at where you are relaxing and have a gentle stretch.
- Over time, you may look forward to coming into this space on a regular basis. As you practise, notice any changes in how you feel in your daily life and how you cope with the ups and downs.

NB If at any time you feel uncomfortable during this exercise or something unsafe begins to intrude into your imagination, just open your eyes and do the emergency breathing or grounding exercises in **Rescue Remedies** on p28. Resume when you feel calmer or leave it for another time. You may find it easier to use the audio recording and listen to a gentle voice guiding you along the way.

Inner Sanctuary

The following recording will guide you through a safe space exercise to help you create an inner 'sanctuary' in your mind.

 3. **Inner Sanctuary (6 mins)**

Once you get used to visiting your safe place, you will find that you can go there almost instantly and whenever you need to. It will become a familiar and relaxing retreat when life gets difficult, or when you need to find a solution to a problem. You can use some of the other tools in this book while you are in your safe place, so you will be coming back to it again and again!

Soothe myself

What sensations do you find most soothing? Jot down some answers to the following:

- What sounds do you remember to be, or experience now, as most soothing? For example, waves rolling onto a shore, birdsong, a piece of music.
- What are the most soothing sights for you? For example, ripples fanning out on the surface of a pond, a glorious sunset.
- What are the most soothing smells and tastes for you? For example, the scent of lavender, the taste of smooth chocolate.
- What are the most soothing textures for you to feel in your hand or against your skin? For example, smooth velvet, a warm bath, a baby's head.

Repeat the safe space exercise above. When you are in your space, add in some of the favourite, soothing sensations you have identified. For example, imagine seeing a sunset outside the window of your safe room, hearing your favourite, calming music playing, smelling a sweet scent of flowers in the air, feeling the warmth of being wrapped in a soft shawl. Try to include some things to enjoy with each sense – sight, hearing, smell, taste, touch.

A peaceful anchor

Listen to the following audio track to experience a guided visualisation that helps you to discover a mental anchor for peace and calm.

 4. **A Peaceful Anchor (8.16 mins)**

Feed my senses

Do some self-soothing for real, by bringing more of your favourite sensations into your life:

- Listen regularly to calming music or go for a walk to hear your favourite nature sounds.
- Put a drop of your favourite perfume or aromatherapy oil on a tissue, or wander around a rose garden and breathe in!
- Focus on the sensation of stroking the bark of a favourite tree, or walking barefoot on grass.
- Feast your eyes on a favourite picture or stroll round a market and enjoy looking at all the colours and textures.

When you have practised some 'single sense' soothing, create some multi-sensory experiences in your imagination or for real by bringing together pleasing and calming experiences that incorporate seeing, listening, smelling and touching. For example, you could extend your love of the sound of a crackling fire on a winter's day to watching the changing colours in the flames and sparks, feeling the warmth spreading through you, smelling the scent of logs burning and so on.

Note: you can also self-soothe through touching yourself in a loving manner and this will be covered in **Chapter 3. Loving Myself**.

My self-soothing box

Create a self-soothing box to open and 'dive into' when you are feeling stressed. This could be any box, but you may want to cover it in a favourite coloured paper or textured fabric. You can collect small things over time to put in your box – anything that feels relaxing and soothing, for example, a pleasingly shaped pebble or shell from the beach or a stress ball you can hold, an aromatherapy oil you can smell or add to a bath, a picture of a sleeping baby or a beautiful flower, a poem, prayer or favourite lyrics from a song.

Rescue remedies

When you notice you are getting anxious or stressed (often a sensation that begins somewhere in the body), try one or more of the following 'quick fixes' to restore calm.

- Try breathing with an extra long out-breath for a few minutes. Breathe in (through your nose if possible) for a count of 4, and out through your nose or mouth to the count of 8. If this feels too much, try breathing in for 3 counts and out for 6 counts. The ratio of a shorter in-breath/longer out-breath quickly overcomes the problem of rapid over-breathing that can accompany mounting anxiety. Like breathing into a paper bag, an old trick for dealing with panic attacks, this breathing pattern stops the stress response in its tracks and triggers a calming of the nervous system.

- If you sometimes feel light-headed or start to float out of your body when stressed, ground yourself by focusing on your feet. Notice the sensation of the soles connecting with the floor or ground, and the weight going through them.

- You can add to this grounding exercise by imagining invisible cords running down each leg, through each foot, and down into the earth. If you are in a house, imagine the cords travelling down through the floor or floors and then into the earth below. Visualise them going deep down and anchoring themselves into rock. You may then want to visit your safe space for a little while.

- If you feel unsafe walking or travelling out and about, protect yourself with an imaginary cloak. Give it a colour on the outside and a colour on the inside that feel protective for you.

Positive affirmations

When I visualise my protective shelter, I can feel calm and safe, even in a chaotic situation.

Soothing myself with my favourite sights, sounds and colours takes me away from anxiety.

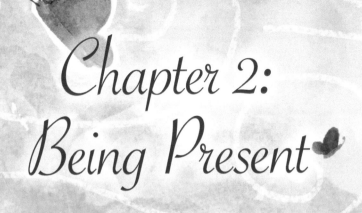

Chapter 2:
Being Present

When I focus on just being present, I can notice how I feel and experience being fully alive.

When we are fearful or emotionally distressed, we can find it difficult to stay focused on 'what is happening now'. We may spend a lot of time remembering how things used to be, wishing we could go back to a time before our lives were overturned by a catastrophic event or we lost our way. We may find that our imaginations run away with us, and we create bleak futures that look even worse than how things seem right now. Living in the past or the future can fuel the fears we feel about the present, and our thoughts can seem out of control as they run around our minds like a bunch of unruly monkeys! Learning how to be calm as each moment unfolds in our lives is a key to recovery and to discovering our inner strengths. By resting in present awareness, we can listen to our inner wisdom. In times of uncertainty, we can even find the answers to our questions from this place.

Being 'present' means showing up for what is going on now, and noticing how we feel in our bodies, minds and emotions. It may mean becoming aware that we are in pain somewhere in our bodies, or that we are thinking negative thoughts, or feeling angry or hopeless – all things we have been trying to avoid. However, dodging or suppressing discomfort requires a lot of struggle and effort, and can become more of a focus in our lives than actually getting on with living. It may lead to unhelpful ways of behaving that temporarily seem to make things feel better, but become problems in themselves, like drinking too much or self-harming. Whatever our avoidance tactics, sooner or later the discomfort will pop up again and increase our suffering. Another strategy we may resort to is going through life on auto-pilot, barely present as we go through the motions of everyday life, keeping the possibility of pain (or joy) at arm's length. The net result of disconnecting from life to avoid discomfort is that we are controlled by it and therefore diminished, unable to express our strengths and personalities through living life to the full.

Acceptance

It may seem counter-intuitive, but staying in the present and accepting how we feel, without trying to change anything, has been shown to reduce the experience of physical pain, depression and anxiety. Sometimes there are things we have to do but feel uneasy about, or surprise situations we find ourselves in that challenge us in some way. These may be a trigger for old, unhelpful reactions that cause us to escape out of the present and go into fight or flight mode (see p11). Our anxiety may then spiral out of control and we can even experience a full-blown panic attack. By staying calmly present, we learn that when we just label and watch our distress, *we are not our distress*; it is a temporary state that we are experiencing and, like everything we experience, it will pass. It doesn't mean that our thoughts and feelings aren't valid, and we may need to act on them in some way. However, we don't have to be at the mercy of them. Being present helps us to learn that we all have a stable and resilient inner core we can trust in when we need to decide how to act.

The key to this mindfulness practice is acceptance; that is, not judging what we are experiencing. As we begin to discover that being with our pain or distress is not as scary as we had imagined, we open to new and more positive ways of living. Coming to terms with things as they are in this way leads to healing on all levels. Even in the most difficult of times, if we pay attention to what is happening within ourselves, we can act resourcefully.

This chapter will help you begin to practise staying in the present and really notice what is happening, moment by moment. When you practise for the first few times, you may want to imagine you are in the safe space you constructed in **Chapter 1**. As your practice becomes more familiar, you can bring it into your everyday life and eventually use it when you find yourself in a stressful or upsetting situation. The more we bring ourselves into the moment, the more we find ourselves staying calm and resourceful. From this place, we begin to feel more in control and able to savour the richness of living and even experience positive emotions like appreciation, wonder and joy. We find we are able to express more of who we really are, freed from the physical, mental and emotional suffering that had come to define us.

> *My job is very demanding and there is a lot of uncertainty about the future of my role. I was starting to take more and more time off sick from feeling stressed and worried about the future. This was spilling into my home life and I stopped doing a lot of things I enjoyed because I always felt rushed and out of time. My relationships at work and at home suffered. A friend took me to classes in mindfulness and I began to practise focusing on my breathing and staying present. When I took the dog for its daily walk, I started to notice my surroundings and everything seemed to calm down for a while. Going back to work, I managed to use my breathing practice to keep my attention on each current task, rather than worry about the changes that might be coming. I seemed to get through more than when I was hurrying before, and I found I could ask for help from colleagues when I needed it. I returned to my hobbies and my energy lifted. I feel like a whole person again, far less anxious about my work and my future. I know that I will cope with whatever happens when it happens.*

Mindful breathing

It is helpful to begin learning to be present by focusing on the breathing. Breathing is fundamentally related to being alive. Its rhythms reflect what we are doing and how we are feeling. It constantly changes, and so it is a helpful way of getting used to change and the need to be flexible. When we are very anxious, our breathing can get faster and faster and more and more shallow. We may feel like we are going to die, as we hyperventilate and even experience a panic attack. For those of us who have experienced this kind of anxiety, it may seem a bit scary to focus on our breathing and we may want to change and control its rhythm. However, with a bit of practice, we can begin to feel much more comfortable with allowing it to be whatever it is, and the more we do this, the more we can experience a calmer way of breathing and being.

Body focus

Feeling the energy within our body can help us to step out of the anxious mind and to be fully present. The activity of fearful thinking subsides and we begin to regain a sense of control. However, when we have suffered trauma or experience anxiety and fear as a regular state, it often seems that we are not fully in our bodies. Being fully and physically present may have proved dangerous in the past and one of our ways of protecting ourselves may have been to use our minds to 'escape' out of our physical form. Another way may have been to 'freeze' in order to make ourselves less visible, just as an animal may do when cornered by its predator. The long-term consequence of these safety tactics is that we may feel disconnected – from ourselves and from others – so that we are not really living our lives. As a result, we may miss many moments of fulfilment and happiness that come our way. Learning to stay with the sensations of our bodies may seem daunting, but with regular practice, even for just a minute or two, we can re-acquaint ourselves with ourselves. At first, we may notice a lot of discomfort and even pain, but by staying with the sensations, we can slowly re-engage with what it is to be fully alive.

Everyday activities

Day-to-day living presents us with a host of activities for mindfulness practice. You can be present in any daily task, it takes no extra effort or time! People often say that truly experiencing each activity seems to make time slow down and give them more space and ease to enjoy their day. Think about brushing your teeth in the morning. It is a chore we tend to do mindlessly, our thoughts on other things, maybe rushing ahead in our minds to getting to work or doing the long list of household jobs that have to be done. We barely notice the present experience, and taking our energy into the future – thinking about other things ahead – makes us feel tired and stressed. We start to rush and that makes things worse. And yet we can create such a different experience when we really pay attention. Every task, however mundane, can become a moment-by-moment sensory delight, providing the space to just be in the moment.

> *During the coronavirus pandemic, I started to wash my hands throughout the day as we had been instructed to. At first, it felt like a chore, and taking 20 seconds each time seemed far too long. Then I decided to use it as a regular mindfulness break and focused on the sensations of pumping soap onto my hands, the sound and glint of running water from the tap, the look and feel of lather rubbing around every part of my hands. My handwashing became an enjoyable time to be fully present – even looking up in the mirror and smiling at myself when I finished!*

The following practices are all ways of learning how to be present by focusing on particular sensations or daily experiences. You can try them all and find one or two that work for you. Your mind will inevitably wander and run off in various directions, again and again.

However, when you notice this has happened, just gently guide your focus back to the present moment and resume your practice. Don't criticise yourself, but rather treat your thoughts and feelings as you would an untrained dog that needs leading back and back again to where you want them to go.

Remember that there are no rights and wrongs to this practice. Just notice whatever is there – sensations, feelings and thoughts – without any judgement. An important element of being present is acceptance and we will be exploring this in more depth in **Chapter 4. Stepping Back and Accepting**.

Now practise

Following my breath

- Sit upright or lie on your back in a comfortable position. Close your eyes if you wish.
- Now begin to notice how the body breathes itself, either by focusing on the belly rising and falling, or the cool air passing in and out of the nostrils. Don't try to breathe in any particular way, just allow your breathing to be whatever it is.
- Maintain your focus on the physical sensation of breathing – on the whole in-breath, and the whole out-breath – as best you can. Your mind may wander again and again, but each time you notice it has strayed, gently guide it back to the belly or the nostrils.
- If it helps, set a timer for one minute so that the practice feels do-able. Once you have practised several times, extend it to 5 minutes and then 10 minutes.
- When you have finished, notice how you feel. Is it any different to before you began?

In addition to setting aside a few minutes of focused practice in this way, you can begin to notice your breathing at different times during the day. Just take your focus to your belly or nostrils during two or three in-breaths and out-breaths. Notice how you are feeling and thinking without any judgement. Over time, be aware of any changes in how you are feeling about yourself.

Breathing with affection

Here is a 10 minute breathing practice with the addition of loving thoughts towards yourself, in preparation for the theme of the next chapter:

 5. **Affectionate Breathing (10.21 mins)**

Watching my thoughts

- Again, sit upright if you can and take a few deep breaths to relax the body.
- Begin to watch your thoughts as they arise, as if they are clouds passing across a sky.
- If a thought hooks your attention and takes you off with it, as soon as you realise this has happened, gently bring your attention back to your breathing for a few moments, before beginning again.
- Don't worry if your mind seems to teem with thoughts, like a stream of heavy traffic on a motorway. As you watch the thoughts, you may eventually discover that there are momentary gaps between them, just as there might be gaps between passing cars. With practice, the traffic may even begin to slow down a bit and the gaps grow bigger. However, the important thing is to allow the stream to be as it is, without trying to make it slow down or to change the nature of the thoughts.
- You may become aware of negative or distressing thoughts passing through your mind. Let them pass by without judgement. Remember that you are not your thoughts.

- Again, you might like to set a timer for one minute, and then extend it gradually as you grow more familiar with the practice.
- When you have finished, notice how you feel. Is it any different to before you began? What has happened to your body, your thoughts and your emotions?

Being in my body

Use the following audio guide to gently scan through your body and begin to notice how it feels. You may want to imagine being in your safe place throughout the exercise (see **Chapter 1**).

 6. **Compassionate Body Scan (30 mins)**

Walking with myself

Sometimes it may feel easier and even safer to move, rather than sit still. You can practise being present by walking a few paces with a full focus on the experience, either in a room or outdoors in a pleasant space. Slow the actions right down, so that you can be aware of all the sensations that arise.

- Stand facing a point about 10 steps away from you, and take a few deep breaths to relax the body. Notice the texture of the floor or ground beneath you and the connection between it and the soles of your feet.
- Slowly raise one heel with the intention to take a step forward. Notice what this feels like.
- Lift the foot and slowly take the step, noticing how the weight is transferred and taken up by the other leg and foot. Notice, too, the feeling of the leading leg swinging forward, and the foot being placed down on the floor or ground again.
- Raise the heel of the other foot and repeat the action of taking a step. As best you can, focus on every sensation in your feet and

legs. You may notice how your arms, other parts of your body and even your clothing get involved in the movement too.

- When you reach the end of your 10 steps, slowly turn around and begin the walk back.
- You can repeat the walk again and again, gently bringing your focus back to the movements any time your mind wanders.

A daily present

Choose a task you carry out most days – taking a shower, washing up, making a coffee, preparing a meal, ironing clothes – and make some notes about all the sensations it involves, what you see, what you hear, what you smell and taste, how you move, and so on. Each time you do this task, be fully involved in it. Notice some new sensations and add them to your notes as you experience the activity in a wholly present way. How did it feel, compared to before? What did you feel when you had completed it?

Remember that walking or travelling to an activity can be an unexpectedly pleasurable experience if you are fully present. Rather than rushing with head down, you can really sense the surroundings and enjoyable sensations that may otherwise go unnoticed – a bird singing in a tree or the sound of friendly laughter, green shoots in the ground heralding the first signs of spring or a clear blue sky up above, the feel of sunshine on your face or a fresh breeze in your hair, the smell of baking bread or coffee brewing in shops as you pass by.

A mindful meal

Experiment with eating your first few mouthfuls of a meal in a completely focused way. Take a few deep breaths to relax the body before you start. Begin with a tiny amount of just one food that is on your plate. Look at it and notice its colour, texture and other properties. Bring it near to your nose and notice how it smells. Place it in your mouth but don't start chewing! Instead, allow your mouth to register its temperature and texture. Then begin to chew very, very slowly, moving it around your tongue and savouring the qualities of taste – sweetness, sourness, saltiness, bitterness. Finally, allow it to slip down your gullet and notice the sensation as long as you can. Now, choose a different piece of food from your plate and repeat the process. What did you notice about these foods that perhaps you have not noticed before? Does your food taste different or better than before?

Eat the rest of your meal with less speed and more attention, enjoying each mouthful in a new way.

Rescue remedies

- To calm the mind and come into the present, focus on your hands. Feel the sensations of energy and aliveness within them and how it increases with your awareness.
- When you are in a stressful situation, bring your attention to your belly rising and falling with the breath and stay with the sensations of the body breathing as best you can.

Positive affirmations

When I watch my thoughts and accept them being there, I notice how my mental activity begins to slow down.

Staying present allows me to watch my thoughts and feelings and to let them pass, without reacting to them.

When I pay attention to an everyday task, I come fully into the present and experience the joy of living.

Chapter 3:
Loving Myself

Learning self-compassion helps me to be gentle on myself and kind to others in difficult times.

When we are lonely or afraid we can often notice that we aren't very kind to ourselves. For a whole variety of reasons we can blame ourselves for things going wrong, put ourselves down if we feel we have failed or made a mistake, or somehow expect that we should be able to manage or cope better than we actually are. In spite of difficult situations that are beyond our control, we chastise ourselves and feel guilty for our shortcomings, adding insult to injury. But does having this sort of attitude to ourselves actually help us when we are suffering? Is there a way of coping that is more constructive and that contributes positively to our self-care?

What is compassion?

We call the capacity to connect with another's suffering 'compassion'. Compassion is an awareness of the suffering in ourselves and others, but also the intention and desire to bring us out of suffering. Being compassionate involves particular qualities and skills. These include noticing that there is suffering and attending to this; understanding what might be causing the distress, or at least being curious about it; being able to empathise or to some extent feel or touch upon another's suffering; and finally, taking action to relieve that suffering. So we can recognise compassion as a capacity we all have to notice the suffering of another and to respond in a loving way. But what about when you are the one who is suffering?

Self-compassion

We all have times in our lives when we make mistakes, fail, or when bad things just happen to us. If a friend or loved one were in the same situation, we would usually respond in a kind way, with soothing, reassuring words, a gentle touch or a hug. However, it would seem that when we are suffering, it is often much more difficult to respond to ourselves with the same level of kindness. This could be due to a multitude of factors but often comes from the messages we have received about ourselves in early childhood, from the culture we are in, or our innate tendencies to protect ourselves from perceived threats. Often there is a harsh inner critic who tells us to "pull ourselves together" or to "stop being so weak!" So instead of being kind to ourselves we amplify our pain by speaking to ourselves in an unkind way or by resisting the situation.

Are we able to notice when we are suffering? As mentioned in **Chapter 2. Being Present**, the ability just to sit with yourself and acknowledge your feelings is the first step, but often this is not easy. We are used to distracting ourselves with activity, or we may have got so accustomed to uncomfortable feelings that we don't even notice them any more. When we become more aware of our own pain and suffering we can start trying to direct feelings of kindness and care towards ourselves. Even though it may feel like we are alone, we all suffer. We are all in the "human-being boat of suffering" together – the fact that we all suffer in our lives connects us, and this theme will be picked up again in **Chapter 6. Connecting**.

> *When I am arguing with my partner over seemingly trivial things I find myself getting upset. By stopping before I react and reminding myself, "This is a moment of discomfort, unease or stress", I can then give myself kindness in that moment. The energy of the interaction changes and doesn't escalate into a fight.*

Having self-compassion allows us to focus our energy and attention on how we might alleviate our pain in a healthy way, and also to activate our soothing system to calm our sense of being under threat and control the systems that are activated when we are afraid or upset.

Activating self-compassion

So how do we turn on or boost this soothing system? We all have this innate capacity to care and love, but it seems that we need to cultivate intentionally the habit of being kind towards ourselves. Compassion is an energetic force that arises from our true nature of love and can lessen, soothe and calm our experience of suffering, as well as help us out of it.

Being present with our thoughts and emotions is not always easy when they are painful. However, what we can learn and practise is 'warming up' our response to these painful experiences and turning towards them with feelings of kindness and compassion. Actively doing this has been shown to reduce the incidence of depression and anxiety and make the experience of 'being human' easier to bear.

The universal triggers for self-compassion are gentle words and tone of voice, soothing touch, physical warmth and a smile! We may have noticed that when someone else is suffering our natural response is to reach out and give them a hug or stroke their back, arm or face. Imagine what your response is to a small child who has fallen over. We can do this for ourselves by just stroking ourselves gently where it feels soothing. This will help to trigger a compassion response. We all have gestures or movements that are self-soothing when we are troubled, but perhaps we hadn't even noticed we were using them.

The soothing system

As we mentioned in the Introduction to this book (p11) our threat/defence and 'doing' systems tend to be overactive for many of us, much of the time, leading to increased anxiety and stress. The *threat/defence* response which protects us from danger, can generate the difficult emotions we may be struggling with – fear, anger and anxiety. In turn, when our thoughts and feelings are anxious or uncomfortable, we can unintentionally continue to trigger the fight or flight response and the release of stress hormones, like adrenalin and cortisol, throughout the body. This can impair our long-term health. Turned inwards, the constant firing of the 'fight or flight' response can lead to feelings of isolation, ruminating thoughts, self-criticism and depression.

The active or *doing* system is a neuro-physiological pathway that gets things done, but is also highly addictive. A lot of our behaviour is driven by the pleasure we get from the release of the neurotransmitter dopamine, which makes it hard for us to stop doing and slow down. It can lead to driven and compulsive behaviours ranging from constantly checking our social media, to gambling, which have a negative impact on our health and well-being.

As we have seen, we have another system – the *soothing system* – that is activated by loving and kind thoughts. It uses the chemical system of oxytocin and endorphins – the 'feel good' brain transmitters. Owing to various life experiences, many people find this system is under-developed. By turning our attention deliberately to cultivating self-soothing, we can move away from being driven by threat or instant pleasure towards self-awareness, self-kindness and connecting with others. Many activities can initiate the soothing system, such as meditation, walking in nature, or creative pursuits. The exercises included in this book are designed to bring the soothing system back into balance through a range of different practices.

Capacity for kind 'self-talk'

The threat/defence response is also triggered by negative self-talk and self-criticism. This negative thinking style often links to difficult emotions and those who are highly self-critical are more prone to depression and anxiety. Often, we may have negative voices in our heads, that 'inner critic' who seems intent on putting us down. Critical voices can come from early caregivers that we have internalised, or from our wider culture or community. Self-criticism will trigger the same stress response as an external threat and, as a consequence, we will 'stress ourselves out'. As a first step towards developing a kinder 'self-talk', it is helpful to become aware of our tone of voice and the language we use when speaking to ourselves. We might notice that words like **should**, **ought** and **must** occur quite frequently as ways of berating ourselves. There may be occasions where they are valid, but more often there will be other ways of looking at a situation and responding to constantly changing circumstances. Although the inner critic has been playing a role in our lives to try and protect us, its judgmental and narrow stance is ultimately self-destructive. Instead, we could consider listening to our kinder, inner self that has a more understanding voice. This part of ourselves can also motivate us to change by being a supportive coach rather than a harsh parent.

> *I would often have a sense of feeling uncomfortable in meetings but I wasn't sure why. As I practised being more self-aware and actively soothing myself, I began to identify an inner, critical voice saying things like, "Don't think you have anything to offer – don't get too big for your boots", and, "They don't like you" – even though there was little evidence for this. I realised these were voices from my early years that I had internalised. Although they had made me feel safe at the time, I no longer needed them. With a lot of love and kindness I thanked them for looking after me in the past, but said to myself that I now have a more supportive voice I choose to listen to.*

A compassionate friend

When it is difficult to extend kindness to ourselves, a first step can be to create an inner compassionate friend. We can remember a time when someone was kind to us or think of a compassionate person we know – what they looked like and how they moved, their tone of voice, what they said, and so on. When we are relaxing in our safe space (**Chapter 1. Creating Inner Safety**) we can bring a similar compassionate presence into that space and experience their caring and kindness. This is the compassionate part of ourselves in action and we can share our fears, thoughts and problems whilst being bathed in kind, non-judgmental acceptance and love.

> *I had a longstanding habit of comfort eating when I felt anxious about something. So when I found myself doing that in difficult times, I created an inner compassionate companion – a wise person who really cared about me. When I knew I was overeating, I would relax in my safe, inner place and invoke them so that I could experience their unconditional kindness. It felt like I could express my feelings without feeling criticised or judged. This soothed me, so my need to eat diminished and with practice, I was able to overcome the habit.*

Another way to connect with being kind to yourself is to think about how you would act if you were looking after a pet you loved. Imagine how you would stroke it, feed it nutritious food, give it exercise, and a nice place to sleep. Now see if you can apply that same care to yourself in your own, everyday life.

Acting compassionately towards ourselves means making choices that will benefit us in the long term and contribute to our physical, mental and emotional health. This may involve self-discipline and changing behaviours, but doing this out of love for ourselves is the greatest motivator. Think of your inner supportive coach saying, "Yes – you can do it!" and remember that love is a greater motivator than fear.

Now practise

What 'system' are you in?

A way of understanding how the innate compassion system operates is to recognise how certain kinds of thoughts and feelings trigger the three main neuro-physiological pathways mentioned above – *threat/defence*, *doing*, and *soothing*. Although each of these systems has a function in our lives, it seems that for most of us, it is out of balance.

Take some time to reflect on how much of your day is spent using each system. Try to represent it in a picture with three circles. A green circle for your *soothing* state, a blue circle for your *doing* state and a red circle for when you might feel under threat, stressed or criticised, either by yourself or others. You may notice that the *threat/defence system* and the *doing systems* are being activated a lot more than the *soothing system*. Perhaps you can go back to this exercise once you have begun to regularly practise some of the self-soothing activities in this book. How does the picture look now? Have you achieved more balance?

Soothing touch

We can use the physiological effect of supportive, soothing touch to trigger the caring system in our bodies, so relax along to this audio commentary.

 7. **Soothing Touch (9.47 mins)**

Alternatively, find your place of comforting touch which will become your anchor for triggering compassionate feelings towards yourself. Begin by closing your eyes and taking a few deep breaths. As you gently stroke yourself, notice what feels supportive, soothing and comforting... Now take your hand and start to stroke your left arm with your right hand... noticing where that feels soothing... then the right arm with the left hand... Give yourself a little hug... Try stroking your face with one hand then both hands, then maybe holding your own hand and giving that hand a gentle squeeze. Put your hand over your heart and send loving feelings through that hand to yourself. Place your other hand on top of that and continue for as long as feels beneficial.

Giving myself kindness

Remembering that challenges and difficulties are part of life and of being human, focus on a time when you suffered and give yourself kindness.

Think of a time when you were upset, had failed or when something bad happened to you. Be aware of any discomfort this memory brings into your body. Now begin by acknowledging this is a moment of difficulty or pain and hold it in your awareness. Be present and stay with it. It may help to name it or to say something like, "This hurts, this is painful..." and then place your hand over your heart or another place of soothing touch for you. Using kind words, say something that is soothing for you such as, "May I be kind to myself, may I give myself love, may I be strong, may I support myself", and then close with a smile. Give yourself the tender energy of an inner smile. You can develop this by using the 'Inner smile' practice below.

Self-compassion break

Relax to this commentary, when you have a problem, for example a difficulty in your relationships, health or work.

 8. **Self-compassion Break (7.43 mins)**

Inner smile

A pleasant way to start the day is to imagine smiling into your body when you first awaken. Smile into your heart, then every part of your body, including your organs. This releases 'feel-good' hormones called endorphins. As you become more practised, you might imagine each part of your body smiling back at yourself!

Write yourself a letter

Writing to yourself from your compassionate voice or as if from a really good friend can help you to overcome self-criticism and cultivate self-love. Think of something you often criticise yourself for and would like to change. Write a letter to yourself from your own inner, kind, compassionate voice, showing that you understand that behaviour and that your compassionate self will support you in making a change.

My compassionate friend

Create a compassionate friend and experience their love by listening to this recording:

 9. **A Compassionate Friend (14.04 mins)**

Alternatively, create your compassionate companion as a figure from fantasy, an animal or symbol – something or someone with a deep commitment to help and support you. In your safe space (see **Chapter 1**), express the worries and feelings troubling you to this compassionate companion, knowing you will not be judged or criticised. Know by their appearance, sound or feel that they have wisdom through experience, warmth, kindness and caring to help you with any problem. Relate to them in a way that feels comfortable for you, for example, looking into their eyes, being held by them or holding them, or talking through your difficulties.

Rescue remedies

- When 'shoulds', 'musts' and 'oughts' come up in your mind, question their validity by saying to yourself, 'Who says?' Maybe the answer to this question will suggest that it is time to let go of them.
- A simple but effective practice is to notice when you are suffering in some way – it could be something like just missing a bus by seconds or having an argument with someone. Before you get caught up in the storyline of what's happening, give yourself kindness through supportive and soothing touch, gentle words and the energy of love.
- If in danger of 'beating yourself up', ask yourself, 'What would my best friend say to me at this time?'

Positive affirmations

I can tune into my capacity for compassion and direct it towards myself.

When I notice that I'm feeling stressed, I talk kindly to myself without judgment.

I give myself permission to meet my needs in a healthy way.

Chapter 4:
Stepping Back and Accepting

Stepping back to observe quietly the storm going on around me, I can respond in more helpful ways.

When we get stressed or thrown back to a time of past hurt and trauma, the emotions of fear and anger can take over from our rational, thinking mind. We may think, say or do things we wouldn't dream of in our calm, logical state and we may act in ways that are at best unhelpful, and at worst destructive. This process of 'emotional high-jacking' arises because the more primitive part of the brain that controls our basic survival instincts takes over from the more recently evolved, intelligent part of our brain, the cortex. The cortex is deactivated when we are emotional, so we cannot think clearly about what we are doing through the mist of rage or rising panic.

The good news is that there are ways we can quickly recover our capacity for clear thinking and action. The earlier we notice difficult emotions arising, the quicker and more effectively we can employ tools to divert and return us to a calmer state. This means knowing how we individually experience the first signs of discomfort. For many, this is a physical sensation, perhaps a rise in heart rate, muscular tension, perspiring or 'butterflies' in the stomach. For others, it may be a general feeling of unease or a persistent thought that something bad is about to happen. Knowing and noting our own first signs provides the opportunity to take action.

We have already explored some practices for calming, and this chapter is going to build on these by utilising a wonderful quality of the human mind – the capacity to stand back and witness ourselves. There are a few further practices that incorporate both calming and observing in order to make better choices about how we react to a situation.

Stepping back

Often, we get caught up in other people's emotions, whether a family member or some unknown person posting their views on social media. We can find ourselves responding by getting angry or anxious. Stepping back from others' distress does not mean we don't care. In fact, by calming ourselves and not getting attached to others' emotion, we can more readily empathise with their distress and be a more helpful resource to them.

> *I would often find myself feeling upset or distressed but not really sure why. By observing my feelings, going to a safe place inside and observing my feelings, I could handle them more easily and understand what was underneath them. I learned that this was a better way to meet my needs.*

Stepping back from difficulties to observe ourselves (and others) calmly can help us to manage our emotions in a number of important ways:

- It can prevent escalating our own emotions to a point where we 'lose' our sense of ourselves and act in unrecognisable and unhelpful ways.
- We can observe and name what is happening to us, which is the first step to acceptance and change.
- We can distract ourselves away from our emotions into helpful behaviours.
- We can avoid getting attached to others' emotions (and this may be helpful to them, as well as to ourselves).
- We can begin to learn and rehearse how to respond differently in difficult situations, and this gives us choices.

> ' When we were in the thick of the Covid-19 situation, I began to feel very fearful about my own and my children's futures, and couldn't see how things would ever get better. I noticed that this would start with my breathing becoming faster and a feeling of unease in my stomach. Noticing these signs as soon as they began helped me to stop my fear escalating. I found two things helped. One was putting on some music and dancing round my room, and the other was phoning a close friend who I knew was always there for me. Over time, I began to get things into a more helpful perspective and to live each day to the full, without fears about what might or might not happen. I can see more possibilities in this difficult situation and this gives me hope. '

Naming and accepting our responses

Naming and accepting our thoughts and feelings is another helpful step in the process of standing back. We often struggle with our own negative thoughts and feelings, using our energy and time resisting or avoiding them, because we don't like or want them. This can be a constant drain on our energy and inhibits our enjoyment of life. In fact, fighting anxiety can add fuel to the flames and may overwhelm us. Naming and accepting what is happening takes away the suffering, as we find ourselves moving towards a more natural level of discomfort.

When we stand back, we are in a position to accept what has happened to us, how things are now and how we unintentionally react to events, which is not always in a way that is best for our well-being. For example, we may be able to notice the first sensations of anxiety and the negative thoughts that can escalate this anxiety into panic. We can then say to ourselves something reassuring, like 'Here come those feelings/thoughts of ...... again, I know that they will pass. I've been in this situation before and I am going to be ok'.

Even if we experience a panic attack, we can take the power out of thoughts like 'I'm going to die!' or 'I'm going mad!' by watching them, accepting that we've been there before, and reminding ourselves that they are temporary. We can help ourselves further by saying to ourselves 'I'm having the thought that...' This distances ourselves from any beliefs that we are our thoughts. We can apply this to negative judgements about ourselves too. For example, instead of saying 'I'm a failure', we can say, 'I'm having the thought that I'm a failure'. We can then notice how our thoughts begin to have less impact.

We can use our thinking brain to name or label what is happening, which helps us to stay in a more resourceful mode. For example, we can say, 'Here come the jitters' or, 'I'm doing that self-judging thing again'. By noticing and naming, we learn to see the thoughts and pictures in our heads as what they are – nothing more than language and images passing through, rather than actual threats or rules to be observed. Also, as we practised in **Chapter 2. Being Present**, accepting uncomfortable physical and mental sensations and urges as they arise allow them to come and go without resistance or struggle. There is then the possibility of learning to change our reactions from a place of calm.

I used to experience a growing heaviness in my chest when I became anxious, and sometimes thought I was going to have a heart attack. I began to practise relaxation and as I rested, I turned my focus on to the sensation in my chest. I began to explore it and was surprised to notice how dark it was, almost the colour of a night sky, and how it seemed to grow and pulsate as my anxiety grew. It seemed really solid, heavy and impenetrable like a rock. As I breathed into it, I could see some pinpricks of light like tiny stars. Relaxing more deeply and breathing into this rock, I imagined the stars twinkling more brightly, taking up more and more of the space until my chest was filled with a golden white light. The space felt lighter and lighter in weight and I could breathe more easily. Now, when I begin to sense the first signs of discomfort in my chest, I breathe into that area and imagine it filling with that soothing light.

Seeing the bigger picture

When we step back, we begin to 'see the wood for the trees'. When we are overwhelmed by emotion and are in survival mode, our thinking becomes very limited. We see things with a very narrow focus, as black and white, all or nothing, which is a common feature of anxiety and depression. We lose a sense of perspective, so that our choices and reactions are similarly limited. Stepping back gives us a wider view in which we may see more possibilities and solutions. In fact our brain switches from negative thinking patterns into more positive 'possibility thinking'. Being able to see ourselves in different scenarios allows us to 'try out' alternative pathways, imagining how things might play out.

The observing self

When we begin to step back, we are able to sense that there are the thoughts and sensations we are having, and then there is the 'I' that is noticing them. There is a process of thinking, as well as a process of *witnessing that thinking*. Sometimes this is known as the 'transcendent sense of self'. We can use our observing self to watch our anxiety or distress with curiosity. It can help to 'score' its intensity by applying a scale of 0 (no anxiety) to 10 (the most severe you have ever experienced). This engages the thinking brain and moves us away from being overwhelmed by emotion. It can also help us to notice that perhaps our discomfort is not quite as bad as the last time. We can start to see that there are 'shades of grey' between the black and white of fear-based perceptions, and remember we are not our anxiety.

Tapping into this capacity to witness our thoughts allows us to understand that no thoughts are real threats, dangers or absolute controls on how we behave. We can also put our thoughts 'on trial'. What is the evidence for an unhelpful thought? What would you say to a best friend if you heard them say that? What would a best friend say to you if you voiced that thought? By standing back from the thought in this way, you can see it for what it is and perhaps challenge its truth.

The capacity to witness can also be a powerful tool in changing our thinking and behaviour. When we are relaxed and in a safe, inner space (see **Chapter 1**), we can mentally rehearse reacting more positively in challenging situations – seeing ourselves look, sound, move and act in ways that are helpful and resourceful, as if watching ourselves on a TV screen or in a film. We can even imagine floating into ourselves on that screen to experience what that 'new me' feels like – perhaps more confident, stronger, or lighter in mood. As we practise in this way, the good feelings resonate in our bodies and we can enjoy the emotional 'uplift'.

Now practise

Be aware

Come to recognise the first signs that you are losing your sense of calm. What are they? Are they uncomfortable feelings somewhere in your body? Are they uncomfortable thoughts or pictures in your mind?

Write them down and give each a simple label, so that you can name them when they start to arise. As soon as they do, practise stepping back and observing them.

Practise acceptance

Imagine a situation in which you regularly feel anxious or uncomfortable, starting with something that is not too challenging. Now notice where you feel the discomfort most in your body, e.g. a heaviness in your chest or a knotting in your stomach. Be curious about this sensation, as if you were a scientist examining an unknown phenomenon. Notice its shape and weight. Perhaps it has a colour or even a vibration or sound. Where are its edges? What is its temperature and texture? Is it hot, or cool, smooth or sharp? As you watch, you may notice further qualities or sensations within the sensation. Breathe into it and accept that it is there. Make room for it rather than resisting its presence.

As you breathe, notice how you feel. Is there a sense that you don't need to struggle against feelings of anxiety, that you can let them come and go? Do they begin to change their shape or intensity as you watch?

Step back from chaos

When you feel unsafe or are surrounded by chaos, listen to this audio recording to help you to step back and recover a sense of safety and connection.

 10. **Stepping Back from Chaos (2.47 mins)**

S.O.S. Standing back, Observing, Steering

Use this simple process to stand back, observe what's going on and steer away from negative responses to more constructive thinking.

Step 1

Take a few minutes out by either leaving the situation, or standing back mentally from the scene. You may want to use audio recording **1. Relaxing Breath** on p18 or the rescue remedy 'Create space with the breath' below to calm yourself. You could use one of the positive affirmations at the end of this chapter, or one of you own to calm and soothe yourself, for example, 'I am aware of myself as calm and peaceful' or, 'I know I am inwardly at peace' or, 'I see myself as tranquil and cool'.

Step 2

As you regain a sense of inner quiet, the next step is to re-view the situation, as if you are an onlooker or a detached observer. Ask yourself if the thoughts you are having are ones you wish to keep. Are they taking you towards being resourceful, or only creating unhelpful emotions and reactions?

Step 3

From this more positive place, it is possible to steer your thinking to where you want it to be.

The 'S.O.S.' technique will not always change situations, nor will it necessarily influence how others respond. Sometimes, the only change may be that your own attitudes or feelings change and so you feel relaxed or lighter.

S.O.S. visualisation

The following visualisation takes you through this process in relation to a difficulty you may be having at work. However, you can use it to focus on any situation, whether or not work related.

 11. **S.O.S (7.03 mins)**

My distractions

If you find it difficult to get into your witnessing self when anxiety or anger is rising and your body is mobilising for action, distract your mind for at least 30 seconds to break the chain of the fight or flight response. Distraction will move you quickly away from actions that at best are non-productive, and at worst may be violent or harmful. Different distractions work better for different people. When fearful or anxious, it is difficult to remember what is helpful, so make a list and keep it somewhere you can easily see it when you notice your unhelpful emotions or thoughts increasing. Examples include:

- Phone a friend.
- Walk briskly round the block or do some vigorous exercise like running up and down stair or star jumps.
- Breathe gently in and out, extending the out-breath so that it is longer than the in-breath.
- Count backwards from 300 in 3's or read the words on a page backwards to engage the rational, thinking parts of the brain.
- Start to do something you enjoy and can get absorbed in, like baking a cake, doing some gardening.

Rescue remedies

- When you feel that you don't have any time to create the space to step back from what is happening, use the breath. Breathe in gently and breathe out with a longer breath. When the breath is fully exhaled, just pause for 2 seconds, saying to yourself, 'Pause, pause'. This quickly provides a sense of space within.
- When you feel a surge of anxiety or anger:
  - Physically stop what you are doing.
  - Take a few deep breaths, then breathe slowly.
  - Stop by mentally applying a 'full stop' to your thoughts, and a brake on your emotions. You may even wish to say, 'Stop!' either silently or out loud in a determined way.
  - Briefly stand back in your mind from the situation.
  - Say to yourself, 'I am calm' or use one of the positive affirmations at the end of the chapter, then feel the calmness beginning to flow through your body and mind.
  - When ready, carry on.
- Rather than say to yourself, 'I am fearful/anxious' or, 'I am angry', say, 'I am having anxious/fearful/angry thoughts'. This brings you away from defining yourself in unhelpful ways.
- When you are beset with difficult thoughts, relax by using audio recording 1. **Relaxing Breath** (p18) and as you grow calm, begin to observe your thoughts coming and going. It may be that you get caught up in your thoughts, but that's ok. Just come back to your gentle breathing and observe again. Imagine that your thoughts are like clouds floating through your mind. Imagine rising above these clouds to a clear blue sky up above. Look down on the clouds but enjoy feeling detached from them.

Positive affirmations

As a calm observer of my thoughts, I can transcend their limitations and see the possibilities for positive change.

When I stand back from my fearful thinking, I can name my responses and put them into a more helpful perspective.

Standing back from unhelpful thoughts, I can quietly observe and then steer towards more positive thinking.

Chapter 5:
Empowering Myself

Getting back in touch with my human capacities
gives me the inner power to face difficulty and create
new possibilities in my life.

When things are uncertain or chaotic around us, often we have the feeling that we are no longer in control. This generates a feeling of anxiety and we become convinced that we can't take care of ourselves. Believing that we are frail, powerless or defective in some way keeps us needing to be rescued. Anxiety forces us to be on the lookout for someone stronger or more capable of taking care of us and we become dependent. We end up feeling like a victim of circumstance and can feel trapped and helpless. As a victim we deny any responsibility for our negative circumstances and, furthermore, deny possession of the power to change those circumstances. We will often look for a rescuer, someone to save us, and if they refuse or fail to do so, we can quickly perceive them as a persecutor. This view of ourselves in relation to others derails our resilience and means we will have real difficulties in making decisions, solving problems, finding much pleasure in life, or understanding our self-perpetuating behaviours. Becoming passive, we believe that things and events happen to us.

How do we come out of this position of being a victim? First, we need to own our vulnerability and take responsibility for ourselves. This means recognising that we do have personal power and can use it appropriately. One way of staying in touch with our power is to see ourselves as someone who creates – whether it is cooking a meal, organizing an event, knitting a jumper, painting a picture, or singing a song. When we affirm our creative humanity, we are more than just consumers. Owning that we do have many powers or capacities that are under our control, can support us to come out of negative behaviours and cope with uncertain or difficult circumstances through our own problem solving and decision making. We can reframe our life story in a more positive light, and create new narratives for our future that are based on our strengths, so that we no longer feel trapped into living out a victim 'script'.

Capacity for forgiveness

There are many moving accounts given by those who have suffered terrible atrocities, about how they were able to forgive the person responsible for their pain. They realised, often much later in life, that the way to free themselves from the pain, anger and resentment of what was done to them, was to forgive. They recognised that forgiveness was an ability they owned and that no one else could give or take away that power – it was theirs to use in any way they chose. Tapping into this capacity to forgive overcame their belief that they had no power over their lives and gave them back their freedom. Their experiences show that although we cannot change what has happened to us, we can change how we relate to it, how to adapt to it and how we respond to it.

Organisations that have investigated processes of reconciliation have also found that victims who had forgiven perpetrators were less angry and distressed than those who did not. Additionally, they were more notably forgiving if they received an apology.

There is a saying, "If we really want to love we must learn to forgive". But how do we forgive? It seems that forgiveness is a process in response to our own aching hearts, breaking the grip of long-lasting resentments and blame, or guilt and shame where we may have hurt others. These feelings have created an armour that protects us, but with the consequence of closing us off from our own hearts. Forgiveness doesn't mean forgetting or accepting bad behaviour, or continuing in an abusive relationship; rather, it allows us to free ourselves from the consequences of bad behaviour. It means acknowledging the pain and suffering in our hearts, and in exploring our deeper feelings, also acknowledging that we have the courage and kindness to recognise our pain. We need to ask ourselves, "Am I ready to face this pain and do I have the inclination to move on from it?"

It takes wisdom to understand the causes of the harm done to us, or the suffering we have caused others, and that it can be the product of a universe of interacting causes and conditions stretching back in time. The process of forgiveness takes patience and time, often years, as we move towards allowing our hearts to soften. It is not an occasional act, but a constant attitude that is part of loving ourselves and others.

The process of forgiveness has a number of stages. The first of these is acknowledging and being aware of the pain; the second is giving ourselves kindness and compassion because the pain is there, no matter what the causes. Third, we need to understand all the different interdependent causes that bought that situation about. Fourth, we have to incline ourselves in the direction of wanting to forgive either ourselves or the other person, understanding that it can take time. Finally, we must take responsibility for protecting ourselves and others so that, if at all possible, it doesn't happen again.

> *As an adult, I realised I was carrying the story of how uncaring and punishing my mother was towards me. It caused me a great deal of emotional anguish. I began to feel tired of feeling like a victim in the situation and decided to set boundaries and stand up for myself. I also became aware of how her behaviour was a result of all the influences in her life, and not to take all of it so personally. I began to forgive her and let go of the negative feelings. Ultimately, I felt I could truly love her and I let go of the negative feelings of the past. This process helped to empower me to cope with other difficulties in my life in a calmer and more resourceful way.*

Capacity for hope

"All shall be well, and all shall be well and all manner of things shall be well" is a celebrated quote by Julian of Norwich. This profound slogan is an invocation of hope that invites us to live more trustingly. When we notice how difficult we find it to accept reality in ordinary life, it calls us to experiment with *letting go* of this resistance and to live without the protection of our judgements – to really trust in that future of all being well, to have hope.

What is hope? It is the ability we have as human beings to project a feeling of what we would ideally like to happen in the future. It is both an emotion and a virtue we can nurture within ourselves. As an emotion, it is characterised by positive feeling about the future, coupled with high motivation, optimism and good mood. Hope allows us to think of an outcome that makes our life better in some way. This can help to make the present situation more bearable but it also motivates us to take action to make it happen. Envisioning a better future as if it were already here is a powerful practice that can make us feel more in control and motivate us to take whatever steps we need to take. Hope is one of the strongest motivations. Although it is by its nature a forward-looking emotion, its real effect lies in the present. Even in the middle of struggles and uncertainty, it can change how the world seems to us and encourage us out of inaction. Just thinking about something cannot move people to act, only emotion can. The strength of hope itself enables us to surmount obstacles and alter difficulties. Hope is its own best hope and is an energy-giving capacity we can use in difficult times.

We know that hopelessness is a destructive state of mind, often linked to depression. People who feel they have no hope are unable to see possibilities for better times, and are at greatest risk of committing suicide. Learning how to go into deep calm, we can use our minds to step back and create hopeful thoughts that remove the blinkers of fear and despair. You may find helpful some of the practices for changing your thinking in **Chapter 4. Stepping Back.** Even when facing one of our greatest fears, death, we can hope for a good death, without pain, surrounded by those we love or by those who care for us. We may even envisage death itself as a portal to something else that is more beautiful than we can possibly imagine.

As well as being an emotion, hope is an intrinsic human virtue, independent of its realisations, an end in itself. It is a positive attitude full of possibility and aspiration. Other values or qualities that also lie within hope are optimism, enthusiasm, determination and patience. Hopeful people have a positive energy and an awareness of their inner values, which they demonstrate in action. They tend to be encouraging, cheerful, confident and inspiring. They are highly motivated people who tend to have a sense of purpose and who persevere in difficult situations. For that reason, we discover much more about a person when we learn about their hopes rather than their accomplishments, because their hopes are a reflection of what they would wish to be. Having hope is fundamental to being human. Hope is like a spark in the darkness, a moment of light, just enough to reveal the path ahead and ultimately the way forward.

> *I recall a time when I felt so low after the break-up of a relationship that I really couldn't see the point of continuing to live. I had lost hope... I began to set very simple goals for myself to experience some satisfaction in completing them, like small cleaning tasks. Instead of feeling sad, I reframed it as 'feeling quiet'. I would take time to immerse myself in one beautiful thing a day just looking at a single flower, a cloud in the sky or a tree. I reminded myself regularly of the phrase, "This too will pass", and slowly my hope returned.*

Capacity for gratitude

We have often heard the question, 'Do you see the glass half full or half empty?' Does it make a difference? There have been many studies that have shown the numerous physical and psychological benefits of our ability to appreciate the good things that life has given us. These range from decreased stress, depression and anxiety through to improved immunity and lower blood pressure. Practising gratitude certainly has the effect of increasing positive emotions. There is also a lot of wisdom in gratitude when we notice how many interdependent factors contribute to our happiness, and how gratitude connects us to so many. Is there a difference between gratitude and appreciation? Gratitude is an emotional response to a gift freely given, while appreciation is recognising that something is valuable to you. Both practices are important to empowering ourselves. Being appreciated is one of our psychological needs, as are being understood and validated, so when we appreciate someone or something we are recognising good qualities and enhancing our relationships with others. We can also feel appreciation for ourselves – acknowledging our own good qualities and our values. Sometimes we can struggle with this, but we are not saying we are better than anyone else, just recognising that everyone has some good qualities – including me!

> *During the coronavirus lockdown, a friend told me about how she passed an old man on the street. He asked how she was and she replied that she was alright but getting a bit tired of all this. He replied "It's good to be here to be getting tired of it. It's just good to be here." This has stayed with me and helps me to regain my sense of appreciation when I feel frustrated with all the restrictions.*

Capacity to set boundaries

When we talk about self-compassion or being kinder to ourselves often it seems focused on the softer side of our nature – the soothing, comforting, validating qualities of our being. However, another aspect of caring for and empowering ourselves is when we are acting in the world, and we need to protect, provide or motivate ourselves. This involves setting boundaries and is just as important as the soothing aspects of being kind to ourselves, although it is more challenging. Our baseline of how we feel is shaped by the early messages we received in life. If these messages were negative, they may have been linked to situations in which someone crossed a personal boundary but we had to go along with them, to keep ourselves safe. Consequently, we may find setting healthy boundaries later in life quite difficult. If we are feeling powerless or victimised in a situation then our self-confidence can be eroded. This may be because the situation has triggered a memory or pattern from the past, often unconsciously. While we might remain unaware of those memories, we know that we don't feel good. If we do assert ourselves that might feel quite scary. Alternatively, we sit on feelings and don't express ourselves. This can lead us to doing or agreeing with things that deep down we know aren't good for us or we really don't want to do. Our self-esteem diminishes as the message we give ourselves is something like, "I don't matter", "I am the bottom of the pile – everyone else comes before me". This is very different to choosing to do kind acts or acting altruistically, which increases our happiness.

A key to setting boundaries is to trust our instinctive response to a request. We need to first notice where that response registers in the body. Is it a niggling feeling in our stomach or a tightening in our chest? When you trust this instinct it's OK to say, "No". Saying no is difficult for most of us. However, we can learn how to say it in a calm, assertive manner, rather than exploding or being rude because we have ignored our own feelings for too long. Posture can often help with this. By maintaining an open, friendly stance and kind expression we are not rejecting the other person and not being unreasonable. Our tone of voice can also help to communicate a calm and steady state of mind. By practising on smaller requests, we can learn the skill of how to say no gracefully. Of course, some people can be very persistent and if we give too many explanations or aren't clear, they will take that as a signal there is room to persuade us to do as they ask. It is best to keep the message simple, clear and repetitive that we are "unable to fulfil this request". Sometimes it is helpful to give ourselves a bit of time before responding to the request, by saying, "I need time to think about that", while we consider whether it is a reasonable request, whether it is something we are able to do without feeling over-burdened, and something we want to do. By giving ourselves this time we will be more able to give an honest, meaningful answer, and also deliver it in the manner we feel comfortable with. In fact, when we are in our own strength, the energy behind setting a boundary is clear, strong and full of self-respect. This is real self-care, where we place our own needs on the same levels as the needs of others including ourselves in the wider circle of compassion that embraces all living beings.

To summarise, empowerment embraces the capacity to change our internal story so that we can challenge unhelpful beliefs and forgive ourselves past mistakes. We can learn to talk more kindly to ourselves and think more hopefully about the future. Learning to be grateful about what we have and how we are right now, and setting boundaries around what we can and cannot do, are important practices that brings us into our power.

Now practise

Re-writing my story – a new perspective

Relax into your inner safe space (see **Chapter 1**) and imagine seeing your whole life story stretched out before you. Walk into your story with a curiosity about your feelings and how they connect with the way you think and behave now. Honestly examine the storylines you have made up about your struggle, then challenge these beliefs and assumptions as if you were a kind friend. This will help you to challenge the beliefs and assumptions you have made about yourself and the power or lack of power you have to determine your life. What beliefs have you put in place to protect you, but which are constraining your choices? What needs to change if you want to lead a more wholehearted life? Write a new story based on the key learnings from the revelations. Use this new, braver story to change your perspective on life and how you engage with the world (see Chapter 1, p23–25).

Experiencing hope

Listen to the following commentary to experience walking a path towards hopefulness.

 12. **Pathway of Hope (4.17 mins)**

Make an apology and free yourself

We all make mistakes and act in accordance with many influences, some beyond our control. However, one thing that often helps people to forgive is receiving an apology. How might you apologise if you have caused pain to another? This might seem like a very difficult thing to do, but it can be made easier by remembering a time when someone apologised to you and how that made you feel. An apology is not telling others we feel sorry they are angry; it is telling them we understand why they are angry with us, and that we regret making them feel that way, and want to remedy the situation. Put together the three parts of a good apology by making some notes in response to each:

- Admit my responsibility.
- Sincerely demonstrate my concern and understanding of why the person is hurting.
- Do something to remedy the offence or prevent a repetition of it. This might even be promising not to do it again.

Then consider how best to deliver the apology – whether in writing, by calling or in person. If the person has died, we can still write down or offer this apology. To apologise for hurts you may have caused can help others to do the same.

If you are not ready to take this step, try writing a letter of forgiveness to yourself as if from a good friend.

Forgive yourself and others

Asking for forgiveness and forgiving ourselves demonstrates the compassion and humility of being human. Listen to the following recording to explore seeking forgiveness for a hurt you may have caused another person and the feelings of shame or guilt you may feel. You can also experience forgiving another who has wronged you and letting go of any emotions of anger or resentment. This meditation can be repeated using different situations. Make sure you allow time to reflect on how you are feeling following your listening experience.

 13. **Forgiveness (6 mins)**

A gratitude journal

Keep a gratitude journal that you can write in at the end of each day, remembering both small and bigger things that you have been grateful for in the course of that day. You could make a list of several things – rain watering the garden, a lovely cup of coffee, a phone call from a friend, completing a task, etc. You may find you sleep better and going back and reading your list will lift your spirits!

Say thank you

In your relationships, thanking others for helping you or making your life better or easier enables you to focus on the value of others. This can be a spontaneous act, for example, thanking people for an event and their generosity in giving you their time. It could be a more considered thank you to your friends or family members for being there for you at a difficult time or during an important part of your life. Try to be specific about what they have done and the way they have done it, and the positive effect this has had on you. You could write a letter to thank them and appreciate their qualities or make a personalised gift. Receiving an unanticipated thank you in this way can feel extra special for both the giver and receiver.

Expressing deep gratitude

As we learn to express our gratitude more readily, we can take our appreciation down below the surface to deeper levels. In order to practise this, start with a simple object. Take a piece of fruit, an apple say, and put it in front on you. If you don't have one, picture it in your mind.

Observe its colour, shape and texture, and give thanks that such a delicious piece of fruit is available for you to eat. Think of someone who may have planted the seed of this fruit, or made the graft for it to start a fruit tree growing. Give thanks to that person, who may live in your own country or far away overseas. Imagine the seed taking root in the earth and give thanks to the nutrients in the earth and to the earth itself. Think of the sun and rain that over the years have helped the tree or bush to grow and flourish. Imagine the tree is in blossom, thank the bees for pollinating and the farmer for their care and attention to all the fruits in their orchard. Thank all the workers who helped to harvest and pack the fruit. Thank the people who transported them to market and then to the shops. Thank the workers who laid out the apples in the shop and the checkout people who sold them. Now see the piece of fruit in front of you and thank all the people who have made it possible for you to eat it. Appreciate its goodness and how it contributes to your nourishment and wellbeing – the smell, the texture as you bite into it and its lovely taste, maybe even the sensation of juice running down your chin! Give thanks for the variety of food that is available to you, and especially for this special piece of fruit.

Perhaps this exercise helps you to see how gratitude can gradually deepen into a practice that you can extend to other objects, events and people in your life.

Rescue remedies

- If you feel you have messed up in some way or failed at something, ask yourself, "What would my best friend say to me?" Consider what you would say to a good friend if they were going through the same situation. This may help you to appreciate the bigger picture and to let go of any negative feelings about what you have done.
- When you notice that you are being triggered by someone else's behaviour, consider other perspectives on the situation. Ask yourself, what would allow you to see this story in a different way? How could you re-write the story so it no longer triggered negative emotions in you?
- Say 'thank you' in response to small acts of kindness from others. Notice how it makes both them and you feel good.
- When faced with a request that you don't feel good about, try saying you'll think about it and give the person (and yourself) a timeframe for a decision. This gives you a chance to calm down and think it through before responding.

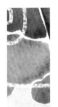

Positive affirmations

I gently open the door of my heart and make space for forgiveness.

I breathe in the possibility that 'all will be well'.

I trust in my ability to express difficult things in a way that inspires and empowers others.

I am stronger than I think. I make me!

Chapter 6:
Connecting

I stay connected to my innermost strengths and values, and connect outwards to something greater than myself, so I am fully resourced in the most difficult situations.

Our brains are 'pre-programmed' for meeting our basic needs. Some of these needs are essentially physical, like shelter, food, water and safety from external dangers, but many are more emotional and are essential to our well-being on all levels. These include a need to feel secure and in control over aspects of our lives, a need for giving and receiving attention, having loving relationships with others, and being part of a community, a need for meaning and purpose in our lives, as well as personal challenge and fulfilment. We will unconsciously try to meet these needs in ways that we have been taught, or in ways that are most available to us. If we have experienced being nurtured and loved as children, and are blessed with a safe environment, good health and opportunities to grow as adults, we will find ways that enhance our physical, mental, emotional and spiritual well-being.

If we have been neglected or abused as children, or find ourselves in dangerous, restrictive or stressful situations as adults, we may find ourselves indulging in practices and substances that are themselves harmful, but which provide us with immediate, temporary relief. These may include the mis-use of alcohol, drugs, unsafe sexual practices, self-harming, eating disorders, obsessional and compulsive behaviours, and violence towards others. Of course, in the long term, such practices exacerbate the problems in our lives and increase our anxiety and stress. We may come to loathe ourselves, heaping self-blame upon feelings of worthlessness and losing the sense of our positive qualities in the process. This means that we are even less likely to respond to challenges in resourceful ways, that is, in ways that cause us to dig deep within ourselves for inner strength, and to reach out for the support of a loving community or presence beyond ourselves.

Connecting to ourselves

Identifying and understanding the resources we have within and outside ourselves can help us to find balance and stability in order that we can begin to meet our needs in healthier ways. Connecting with who we really are puts us in touch with the unchanging, spiritual aspects of ourselves – our values and personal strengths. Research in the field of positive psychology has shown that identifying and using our particular strengths – our 'signature strengths'– help us to create positive emotions, improve our well-being and help make our lives more authentic and fulfilling. While eating an ice cream on a hot day may give momentary pleasure, showing our kindness by helping someone in need can provide a longer lasting senses of gratification. These 'interior' resources help us to learn, grow and heal. They are enduring traits that can be strengthened through practice and perseverance.

The path to understanding ourselves and drawing upon our inner wisdom can come from the process of creative pursuits – poetry, art and gardening, for example – and many other activities during which we withdraw from the drama going on around us and the chaos of thoughts in our minds. In the silent space that such activities create, we can emerge as our unique, enduring self, beyond rational thought or analysis. In turn, we can connect outwards to something bigger than ourselves which provides a sense of belonging, whether this be to a community, our natural environment, universal energy, or a divine source. We may belong to a religious or spiritual community that helps us to connect deeper to the spirituality within. Meditation and prayer are both ways of making this deeper connection. Meditation in particular can be quickly learned and practised anywhere, and if done for even just a minute, can connect us with our essence and with something beyond. Connecting to ourselves as spiritual beings is further explored in **Chapter 7. Discovering Inner Peace and Wholeness**.

Play

We can spend much of our lives hiding our true selves away under layers of roles we play. These roles have expectations put upon them by others and can constrain our ways of behaving and expressing ourselves. Setting these aside and learning to be playful is a route to connecting to ourselves and others on a deep and resourceful level. Watch children play and notice how they live in the moment, without expectations or the self-consciousness of how they might appear to others. Also, they laugh a lot. We know that laughter is a great all-round healer. Seeing the lighter side of life can provide us with a sense of relief and release when things just seem too much to bear.

> ' *When I feel fearful, I watch my little grandson playing, oblivious to my observation or to what I might expect of him. I join him on the floor and allow him to lead me into his creative world, where an empty box becomes a bus that hoots or a sofa becomes a mountain to climb. We act out simple events and make noises as we do so. Minute by minute, he changes his focus and I find myself crawling, dancing, singing and hiding. We share our laughter and fun and I feel that I have released my inner self and given myself permission to play.* '

Connecting to others

Connecting to others can provide invaluable support in times of uncertainty and anxiety. Belonging to a community – whether your family, your local neighbourhood, or a group based on shared interests or beliefs – can provide a safety net and source of mutual support. Reaching out and asking for help can be difficult for those who have spent a lifetime caring for others. This is why developing self-compassion is so important, since it provides the foundation stone for self-care, including seeking support (see **Chapter 3**).

It is a gift for those called upon to feel they can respond to another's needs, helping them to feel wanted and valued. Sometimes, we may feel we are in such difficult circumstances that we cannot help others, and that is ok. However, we may find that even giving a little of ourselves in service to others can begin to turn us around and allow us to grow a little stronger. Fear and uncertainty can play into our self-protective instincts, and cause us to distance ourselves from others. Moving away from self-centredness towards altruism can occur as an immediate response to suffering around us, or can emerge gradually as we begin to tap into our inner strengths.

> *I was having to self-isolate for a very long period during the Covid-19 outbreak. I was consumed with my own fears and was withdrawing from contact with others. I turned to over-eating for some comfort, but that just made me feel even worse about myself. One day I was invited to join a social media group of neighbours down my street. Their postings of jokes, happy and sad moments, and offers of help made me feel I was not alone, and that others shared the emotions I was feeling. Eventually, I offered to join an initiative making protective masks for local healthcare staff. I love sewing and a neighbour dropped me off the supplies I would need. When I sat quietly sewing, I felt purposeful again, connected to my neighbours and able to make a contribution to my community.*

Connecting to nature

Connecting to nature is known to be highly restorative on all levels. The natural world has its own resilience. It passes through the seasons with unfailing dependability, giving us different gifts to notice at every stage – colours, blossoms, flowers, fruits, insects and animals. It is also able to recover with amazing ease. Go for a walk in nature as often as you can. Listen to the sounds and look at the beauty around you. Breathe in the scents and feel the ground under your feet. If you cannot get out, listen to audio track **15. Creative Garden** below or audio track **20. Four Seasons** in Chapter 8.

However we choose to make inner and outer connections, the growing knowledge of the resources we have within and around us can help us to develop resilience to weather any storm. As we come to understand that we are all connected and interdependent, our strength and compassion can begin to make their contribution in the world.

Now practise

My inner values

List the values and strengths you feel you have most exhibited in your life, particularly in challenging situations. A value is a quality that guides the way in which you act, rather than what you do. Examples might be determination, courage, optimism, loyalty, co-operation, flexibility. If you find this difficult, think of a time when you were challenged but managed to find a way through. What values and strengths did you show in the way that you handled the difficulties you faced? Alternatively, you can listen to this audio track to allow your inner values to emerge without conscious thought.

 14. **Experiencing Personal Values (5.06 mins)**

Now make a list and highlight the top three values.
For each value, describe it in different ways, by imagining it as follows:

- As a flower or plant.
- As a sculpture.

- As a landscape.
- As a person.

My creativity

Experience your own inner creativity and wisdom with the following track:

 15. **Creative Garden (11 mins)**

Following your listening, you may wish to draw any shapes, colours or images you found yourself creating during this visualisation.

My external resources

It's important to know where your sources of support are for you to connect into during difficult times. These could be individuals, groups, communities or a more spiritual and divine presence.

Who would you turn to in the following circumstances?

- When you are feeling scared.
- When you are feeling low.
- When you have made a big mistake.
- When you have had bad personal news.
- When you have fallen out with a family member or close friend.
- When you have been bereaved.
- When you have been on the receiving end of bullying or violence.

Now consider where the gaps are in your support?
How could you fill those gaps by connecting beyond yourself?

How can I help?

Sometimes, it may seem that we have nothing to give. However, consider these ideas and find one thing each day that you can do to be of service, however small. Small acts of kindness, looking after someone or something beyond yourself can help you feel more positive and empowered.

- Plant some seeds or a plant and look after them as they grow.
- Give your pet an extra few minutes' stroking at a stressful time of day.
- Smile at someone who is helping you and thank them.
- Write or send a letter to someone you haven't seen in a long while telling them why you value them.
- Leave some flowers from your garden on a neighbour's doorstep.
- Pass on a good book to a friend.
- Have a clear out and donate your unwanted things to charity.
- Offer to do some shopping for someone who is unable to go out.

Rescue remedies

- When you feel disconnected from others, phone a friend and ask how they are. Just listen, rather than tell them about your problems and worries.
- Watch how a child in your family plays, or better still, join in and set aside any expectations about how you would normally behave.
- When you awaken feeling unfulfilled or needy, select one of the personal values you have identified. See to what extent you can bring it into both this moment, and to the rest of your day.

Positive affirmations

When I connect to the strengths within myself, I let go of my feelings of fear and act resourcefully.

When I create or play, I get in touch with my innermost self.

Reaching out for help deepens my connection with others.

Offering help is a way of putting myself in touch with my own strengths.

Chapter 7.
Discovering Inner Peace and Wholeness

When I go into silence, beyond my thoughts and feelings, I connect with my spiritual self

In the previous chapters we have gone on a journey through creating a safe space for ourselves; being present in the moment; being kinder to ourselves; stepping back from our thoughts and feelings and accepting ourselves; and empowering us with capacities for hope, gratitude and forgiveness. But where is this journey leading us? We are travelling inwards, through the storm, to the eye – that place of complete stillness and calm.

Inner peace is the key to developing a more positive attitude towards ourselves and our lives. It strengthens us psychologically, bringing about an enhanced sense of well-being and meaning to life, and allows us to access our own wisdom. We catch glimpses of this inner peace when listening to a mountain stream or the sound of a bird singing. In order to be really present to these experiences our mind needs to be still. When it is, we may sense something deeper, beyond words – a kind of thought-less awareness of beauty and truth, our inner essence. Being able to travel to this place is the journey of meditation.

We have talked about our ability to observe our thoughts and the capacity we have to learn to watch ourselves doing things or to have conversations with ourselves. We have also explained the effect of certain kinds of thoughts and emotions on our brains and the chemical pathways they trigger. However, somehow this never fully answers the question of *who* it is that is experiencing our lives. *Who is the experiencer?* We have thoughts and feelings but who is generating them? We may come to understand there is an essence within that transcends our outer identity and all the roles we play in life.

The spiritual self

The *spiritual self* is a subtle energy that is different from the brain and its cognitive activities, yet it can express itself and gathers information about its surroundings through the physical senses and brain functioning. This is the spiritual being that is experienced when people have near death or 'out of body' experiences, where they can look down on their bodies while still feeling whole and complete. Essentially this spiritual self is the awareness that recognises itself to be 'I', the experiencer, the observer. Sometimes we call it the *watching consciousness* or *spirit* or *soul*. An important distinction here is not that I _have_ a soul but that I _am_ a soul, a spiritual being. This perspective brings a wholly different dimension to our experience.

> ❜ During the Covid-19 lockdown, initially I felt anxious and fearful. As I discovered the new quiet around me, and the time and space I had to just be still, I began to experience a 'silver lining' to the situation. I was able to reflect on who I really am and what is really important in my life. My priorities have changed and I don't want to go back to how things were before. I want to give more attention to my spiritual self as I realise that this helps me to stay content and more peaceful. ❞

What are my thoughts and feelings?

The energy from you, the soul, carries a vibration that resonates with the outside world and triggers responses from it. These are your thoughts and feelings and are similar to the materials an artist uses. Like the artist, who knows she is not the materials she uses (nor is she the painting), we are not our thoughts and feelings, but something more transcendent. An emotion is an energised thought pattern arising in the place where our mind and body connect, and is a reflection of our mind-in-the-body. Thoughts are experienced as flowing quickly through the mind. Emotions, however, have a strong physical component that is felt in the body and move us to respond in a variety of ways. Usually we find it difficult to stay present enough to be able to watch an emotion as an observer, so it tends to take us over. Through lack of awareness we are pulled unconsciously into identifying with the emotion and it feels as if the emotion is us. We can then spiral into a vicious cycle in which the thought feeds energy to the emotion and the emotion feeds energy to the thought. The more identified we are with our thinking and feelings, the less we are present as the *watching consciousness*. When we are the watcher or the observer, we are not the thought, we are not the emotion, but the creator of them.

Sense of identity

It is especially important in times of uncertainty, when fearful feelings arise, to understand what might be generating those thoughts and feelings and to think about where we derive our sense of identity. Fear and other distressing emotions are usually associated with a sense of loss. Spiritually, the loss of identity is a loss of awareness of who we are beyond name and form, that is, *ourselves as spiritual beings*. It arises out of a sense of threat and the deep fear of feeling abandoned or incomplete. It is an emotional pain that we try to keep at bay by keeping very busy and distracting ourselves with all kinds of external trivialities and activities. We try to compensate for our loss of identity by deriving a sense of self that is based on our physical bodies, our minds and our egos. However, these represent ever-changing states and so we will continue to face loss and consequent anxiety and fear.

As a spiritual being, our natural state of inner connectedness is one of peace, love and joy, subtle but intense qualities that lie beyond our emotions and at a much deeper level. These define *our true nature*, the nature that we occasionally glimpse through the gaps in our conscious thinking. We can experience this state when connected to nature and moments of great beauty, but also at times of extreme physical exertion or even danger. In that stillness where time and external events recede, we can glimpse our spiritual qualities. They are always there, although we may only get a fleeting sense of them in the busy-ness of our day-to-day lives. Having a sense of our inner qualities of peace, love and joy brings a stability to our sense of self that gives great inner strength when facing challenging situations.

Core beliefs

What can get in the way of experiencing our *true nature*? The answer is our beliefs about ourselves. Our beliefs are how we make sense of the world and make meaning from our experiences. They are very personal and intimate, often not spoken about or shared, and sometimes not even known to ourselves. When we are young we may receive conflicting information about ourselves and the world and in trying to make sense of this, we can develop distorted or damaging beliefs about ourselves. We are unable to see the broader picture or understand other people's motives or biases, and so wrongly conclude that there is something wrong with us. It may just be a feeling that we're not good enough, we are a failure or defective in some way. At the heart of these negative core beliefs is the universal need to be loved, and our feeling that if we were different in some way, or behaved differently, we would become loved and loveable. From our lack of understanding, we end up blaming ourselves for causing situations. This may give us a sense of control that is preferable to feeling fearful or unsafe, because we can tell ourselves that if only we were better in some way, everything would be alright. Accepting there are forces beyond our control, or that we can't control other people's behaviour – especially when we depend on those people for our care and sustenance – is very frightening. Negative core beliefs can often pop up at a time in our lives when we feel especially vulnerable or challenged. This is because having learned them so early, they have become habitual. We have grown accustomed to viewing and responding to the world from these unconscious beliefs.

When we shift our sense of identity to encompass ourselves as spiritual beings, we know that at our core there is goodness. Those attributes of peace, love and joy are our innermost nature and were there before the layers of painful experience and suffering accumulated. We understand ourselves to be still, loving, positive energy that is unbounded by the material plane. Our original qualities are our *positive core beliefs*. They lead us on a journey inwards towards 'soul consciousness', whereas our negative core beliefs lead us outwards to dependency and destructive habits as we try to gain love from external sources. The practice of meditation encourages us to gently shift our sense of identity to that part of us which is more stable, lasting and clear, the part of us that we know to be our true selves.

How do we get there?

We may experience glimpses of our true selves in meditation or through other processes that tap into our own inner goodness. These can be creative processes that bypass our thinking minds and use different aspects of ourselves to access this 'higher nature'. If we track a sound back to where it starts what do we discover? Every sound is born out of silence and dies back into silence. Similarly, if we track back a thought or feeling to where it originates, we arrive at the same thing – silence. Everything emerges from stillness and this is the inner journey at the centre of all meditation practices when we experience the peace that lies within us. There are many different practices that can take us beyond our busy, talkative minds into a realm of pure experience, one of stillness, tranquillity and love. It is in this state that we feel deep connection to ourselves, to humanity, to nature and sometimes to a divine energy outside ourselves. In fact, the quest to know or connect to the highest spiritual energy comes as a consequence of recognising the depth of our own inner being. The quality of this energy is often described as an 'ocean of peace', a 'friendly light', or 'unconditional, pure love'. Through meditation, and for some through prayer and other reflective practices, it is possible to connect to this energy and to experience the original qualities within our spiritual being. It becomes a compassionate friend – a source of comfort and strength in difficult times.

Facing death

In times of turmoil brought about by large-scale issues like climate change, pandemic or war, we may find ourselves confronted with our own mortality and the death of others. On a more personal level, death may suddenly loom out of serious illness, criminal violence or accident. On this journey of rediscovering the goodness of our inner selves, we find an inner strength that can be especially useful when facing death or dying. The crises we experience in life can involve witnessing the death of someone we cared for, either professionally or personally, experiencing the grief of losing a loved one, or contemplating the possibility of our own death. As the power to experience deep peace develops, we can allow its calming and healing energy to reach the body as well as the mind. We are then able to become more effective in being with our own and others' suffering and distress. This includes facing the grief of loss, the reality that we all will die, and the fears that attend the process of dying.

As a nurse during the Covid-19 pandemic, I came face-to-face with death on a scale I could never have imagined. In the noisy, stressful environment of the covid ward, I witnessed difficult deaths of both patients and colleagues, isolated from their loved ones who could not be by their sides. During my breaks, I would find a quiet place to take a few minutes to check in with my inner self. Breathing through and quietening my anxiety and fear, I was able to access a more stable, inner peace within. Just a few minutes spent like this re-charged my courage and determination, enabling me to go back to the ward and find ways of extending compassion to those I was caring for.

Knowing, and moreover, experiencing, ourselves to be spiritual beings, can allow us to face our eventual passing and that of others with acceptance and inner peace, even when this prospect has come upon us out of the blue, as for example with a diagnosis of terminal illness. In the process of experiencing ourselves as peaceful beings, we may come to know that we will continue to exist in some way. We may understand that we have constant access to a dimension of silence where we can find a transcendent source of positive qualities. It is this source that fills us and helps us on our journey of self-discovery, even when we, or someone close to us, is approaching the end of physical life.

Looking after my friend who was diagnosed with terminal cancer, we practised a regular meditation to prepare her, the soul, to leave her body and have a peaceful passing. As she slowly lost her physical strength, her world became more focused on her inner qualities of peace and love. She gained a sense of travelling forwards into light and felt welcomed into this other realm. Her fear of death diminished and she connected with the love in each person who visited her in the final stages of her illness. This made the whole process one of calm, dignity and respect.

Reaching wholeness

A sense of connected 'wholeness' is intrinsic to our fundamental nature and when we become aware of it, we can draw on the qualities, strengths and wisdom that lie within us all. Each of us has an original wholeness, present before any damage or scarring that has occurred in our lives. Through silence and meditation, we can reconnect with this at any time. This domain of being takes us beyond any fragmentation, damage, loneliness or suffering. Becoming more familiar with our wholeness, we can be healed and nourished, learning to live without fear, insecurity or even despair. The practices throughout the book, but particularly in this chapter, will help on this explorative journey.

Now practise

Who am I?

The following commentary encourages you to reflect on special qualities you have that are part of your self-identity and beyond your physical being. Have a piece of paper and pen at the ready to jot down or draw any insights that arise.

 16. **Who Am I? (5.43 mins)**

Using the energy of positive thought

We know our thoughts can in an instant take us anywhere, from the hustle and bustle of a busy street to a secluded beach where waves gently ebb and flow upon the shore. In the latter example, we feel an atmosphere of peace. When we think of people we love, such thoughts create a positive feeling in the mind. By creating positive and peaceful thoughts, we can quieten our minds and move towards the silent centre of our consciousness. By thinking deeply about our original nature as beings of peace, love and wisdom, we begin to experience those qualities which may have been latent or hidden.

Practise saying quietly to yourself, 'I am a peaceful being, I am light, I am love….' By creating positive thoughts, you can lead yourself naturally into an experience of peace, inner strength and love.

Moving closer in

When relaxed, follow these steps:

- Begin by just listening to the sounds around you. Bring yourself into the present moment by noticing or adopting an attitude of waiting.

- Bring the focus of your attention closer in – first by observing what's going on in your body, identifying where you are holding onto tension and encouraging that to relax; then onto your breathing, allowing yourself to be soothed by the gentle, rhythmic sensation of breathing in and breathing out, like waves lapping on the shore.
- Coming closer in, observe the thoughts in your mind and any feelings that are arising – just notice them, accept them and let go – like standing by a stream and watching the water flow past.
- Allow yourself to drop deeper into the pauses between thoughts – deeper into silence and stillness underneath thinking and feeling, allowing yourself to sense and then experience your true nature of love, peace and joy.

My inner core of peace

Move beyond your thoughts to the experience of inner peace by listening to this track.

 17. **My Inner Core of Peace (4.25 mins)**

A simple meditation

Use the following track to experience a simple meditation that connects you with the energy of peace and love.

 18. **Simple Meditation (6.50 mins)**

Rescue remedies

- When your mind is racing, just try watching. Ask yourself, 'I wonder what thought I will think next?' Waiting and being present may help you to notice the stillness that lies beneath the thoughts.
- When things around you indoors are noisy or chaotic, being in nature can awaken the dimension of stillness. Try walking outside and tuning into the trees, plants, flowers, birds or insects around you. Absorb yourself in their quiet energy, be present with them and notice inner stillness arising within you.
- When you are distressed and need support, step back and take a few moments to tune in to a higher energy, universal love or whatever you conceive that to be. Take courage and strength from this special connection.

Positive affirmations

When there is stillness within I can hear the voice of my own wisdom.

When I tune into the energy of nature, I resonate with feelings of deep peace.

I am the inner artist – a creator of thoughts and feelings.

I am a peaceful soul – an eternal point of light.

Chapter 8:
Resilience Beyond the Storm

*I become resilient when I am
connected to my whole self.*

What is resilience?

Resilience can be described as a resourceful response to a challenge, or as an adaptation to stress, implying the ability to recover quickly from illness, change or misfortune. It is the ability to 'bounce back' from adversity, to bend and return to one's original 'shape', rather than to break. It doesn't mean that we are impervious to things that befall us. Indeed, we may be seriously affected by trauma and experience a whole raft of psychological difficulties. However, it does mean that we can carry on with our lives, cope with pain and distress, and even grow as we discover meaning in the events themselves.

Recovering from adversity can take us through many emotions and levels of energy. Initially, we may be in survival mode, powered by adrenalin to defend ourselves or others and caught in a maelstrom of anger, anxiety or worry as we try to keep our heads above water. Our reactions may exhaust and deplete us, leading to a sense of hopelessness. Alternatively, we may find ourselves powered by positive energy to make things better, fuelled by optimism and even excitement as we surmount the challenges before us and grow in our confidence. We may cycle between these states, but as when we undertake intense physical workouts, we need to take regular rests to build up our strength. If we push ourselves, we will soon reach burnout. Through calming practice, we can reach a place where we recover or discover what it feels like to be serene, stable, and at ease.

While any storm will eventually pass, we will need to maintain our personal resilience to meet future and unexpected difficulties. It is all too easy to go back to how things were before, retreating into old habits and ways of reacting that may harm our well-being and capacity to stay calm. Additionally, noticing how a storm changes the landscape of our living can help us to make positive changes in how we go about our lives. Recovery and the maintenance of resilience can be greatly assisted by having resilient role models and external supports. However, as we have seen, inner resources like our personal values, capacity for hope and getting beyond our thoughts and feelings to connect with ourselves as spiritual beings, can provide us with the purpose and meaning to prepare for and continue our journey, whatever the weather outside.

The spiritual tools of resilience

This guide has introduced some tools for re-discovering our capacity to calm our threat/defence system and connect with our whole selves, when all around us may be chaotic or uncertain. Through practising the simple activities it contains, we hope that some will become second nature and help you to draw on your resourceful inner strengths through and beyond the storm. Here is a recap of what we have covered:

1. Creating inner safety
Creating a special place of safety within our minds, by using our mental power to visualise, helps us to calm right down and to soothe our minds and senses.

2. Being present
Coming fully into the present moment through mindfulness practice moves us away from fearful thoughts about the future and hands back a sense of control in chaotic times. Most importantly, it enables us to come to terms with things as they are.

3. Loving myself
Learning self-compassion is an important step towards healing the distress of past events, accepting myself as I am, and developing compassion for others.

4. Stepping back and accepting

Learning how to stand back from the drama of life and witness our own thoughts and actions puts difficult events into perspective and frees us to respond resourcefully, rather than from a place of fear or panic.

5. Empowering myself

Expressing who we truly are and forgiving ourselves and others gives us the power of agency so that we can begin to act with hope, purpose and determination.

6. Connecting

Connecting deep within and beyond ourselves helps us to identify our inner and external resources that we can draw upon in difficult times.

7. Discovering inner peace and wholeness

Through meditation practice, we can discover a sense of inner peace and wholeness to quieten any sense of turmoil on the inside.

Resilience in the face of suffering

One particular challenge to our resilience is how we respond to our own and others' suffering. When we find ourselves in chaotic and uncertain times, we can become stressed and off balance. We can withdraw from others as our actions become focused on our own protection and sustenance. This is a natural response to meeting our human needs, but it can result in selfish, greedy and competitive behaviour. Practising self-compassion helps us to quell the anxiety we may experience and move beyond that 'little self' who is afraid.

Our sense of inner calm may be sorely tested in the face of others' suffering. Particularly if we find ourselves in caregiving situations, the expectations and difficulties of another can weigh heavily upon us. In trying to help, we can take on another's emotions or fears. We lose the sense of our own self and our inner equanimity. We become unable to evaluate our own and others' needs. From our practice of self-compassion (see **Chapter 3**) can arise the capacity to extend compassion to others, even where we are unable to help them.

One of the positive outcomes of largescale disruption, such as climate catastrophes and pandemics, is that we begin to recognise our interconnectedness. We often witness acts of courage and altruism towards others that go far beyond any consideration of personal safety and well-being. As we witness people's suffering near to home and across the planet, we may experience distress at not being able to help in any direct way. However, by stepping back, we can restore our own sense of stability and calm, in order that we can send a flow of love and compassion to others, wherever they may be.

> When our country was going through the peak of the coronavirus pandemic, I began to feel isolated and afraid. I saw people undertaking heroic work in our health and support services and felt frustrated that I couldn't help. By practising self-compassion I restored my sense of calm. Standing at the front door clapping for our key workers made me feel connected to my neighbours and was an opportunity to show my appreciation for those making such sacrifices on behalf of us all.

Some concluding thoughts

A sense of interconnectedness helps us to reach out to others – family, friends, community, when we need support to remain resilient. When we each 'get behind' the other, we can tackle adversity as a team and help each other to remain determined and courageous.

Times of upheaval and trauma can drive divisions between ourselves as individuals, groups and countries. Defending our own corner can lead us down a path of discriminating or disempowering others, whether on the basis of personal characteristics like gender and ethnicity, or nationality. When we learn to live in our own wisdom, we can begin to recognise our commonality, that we all have an innate goodness, and that any toxicity in what others say and do comes from ignorance and fear. We can learn to live from a place of acceptance and love, and rest in an awareness that nothing is certain, but that we can trust in our 'spiritual shelter'.

Finally, in challenging situations we can turn to and draw strength from something greater than our own being, for example we can turn to a universal energy, or divine source of being (see **Chapter 7**). Then we become our whole selves and can bring our best to any situation, knowing that our contribution can make a difference.

Now practise

Checking in

In order to build and sustain personal resilience, we need to regularly 'check in' with ourselves to see whether we feel out of balance – physically, mentally, emotionally or spiritually. By doing this we develop our self-awareness and responsibility for taking action to restore our well-being. We can mindfully respond, moment by moment, to threat and changing circumstances, rather than mindlessly reacting from a place of fear. Turning inwards helps us to recognise and draw on our inner strengths when difficult times come around again, and cultivating hopeful thoughts and a clear intention can strengthen our determination to ride the storms of our misfortune.

Here is a recording for suggested daily practice that encourages you to 'check in'. It combines body, breath and thought awareness to take you to peace and stillness within.

 19. **Soft Landing (11.43 mins)**

Resilience through nature

Consider the strength and resilience of a plant or tree as it weathers the seasons that come and go. However, slender, it seems to adapt to the changing conditions and bend with the worst of the weather, rather than staying rigid and eventually breaking. Use the following commentary to experience being a plant or tree as it experiences a year in its life.

 20. **Four Seasons (8.52 mins)**

What did you notice about the way you felt about yourself afterwards? What particular strengths do you identify with?

Positive affirmations

I can respond flexibly to adversities that come my way.

When I respond to the suffering of others, I can move beyond my own difficulties and feel that we are all connected.

I am a peaceful, resilient person.

Practices acknowledgments

The practices **'Soothing Touch'** (p43) and **'Self-compassion break'** (p44) are reproduced with kind permission of Guilford Press from *Mindful Self-Compassion program* developed by Chris Germer and Kristin Neff. https://centerformsc.org/

Audio recordings acknowledgments

The commentaries marked with an asterisk are shared by kind permission of Guilford Press. They are from the *Mindful Self-Compassion program* developed by Chris Germer and Kristin Neff. https://centerformsc.org/

The rest of the recordings are reproduced with kind permission from the Janki Foundation for Spirituality in Healthcare

Introduction

1. Relaxing breath spoken by Craig Brown (from *Lifting Your Spirits*)
2. Breathe and relax spoken by Lucinda Drayton (from *Happidote*)

Chapter 1

3. Inner Sanctuary spoken by Matthew Stephenson (from *Values in Healthcare*)
4. A peaceful anchor spoken by Gopi Patel (from *Values in Healthcare*)

Chapter 2

5. Affectionate breathing spoken by Sarah Eagger *
6. Compassionate Body Scan spoken by Sarah Eagger *

Chapter 3

7. Soothing Touch spoken by Sarah Eagger *

8. Self-Compassion Break spoken by Sarah Eagger *
9. Compassionate Friend spoken by Sarah Eagger *

Chapter 4

10. Stepping back from chaos spoken by Samantha Fraser (from *Happidote*)
11. S.O.S spoken by Sarah Eagger (from *Values in Healthcare*)

Chapter 5

12. Pathway of Hope written and spoken by Jan Alcoe
13. Forgiveness spoken by Craig Brown (From Dr Craig Brown's *Mindfulness podcast series*)

Chapter 6

14. Experiencing Personal Values spoken by Sarah Eagger (from *Values in Healthcare*)
15. Creative Garden spoken by Jan Alcoe and Arnold Desser (from *Heart of Well-being*)

Chapter 7

16. Who Am I? spoken by Gopi Patel (from *Values in Healthcare*)
17. Settling into my inner core of peace spoken by Lucinda Drayton (from *Happidote*)
18. Simple Meditation spoken by Sarah Eagger (from *Values in Healthcare*)

Chapter 8

19. Soft Landing and My Inner Sanctuary spoken by Sarah Eagger *
20. Four Seasons spoken by Matthew Stephenson (from *Values in Healthcare*)

Lifting Your Spirits: seven tools for coping with illness www.jankifoundation/lifting-your-spirits/
Heart of Well-being: seven tools for surviving and thriving www.jankifoundation/the-heart-of-well-being/
Values in Healthcare: a spiritual approach www.jankifoundation/values-healthcare-spiritual-approach/
Happidote www.jankifoundation.org/happidote/
Mindfulness for Everyone podcast series by Dr Craig Brown www.jankifoundation.org/mindfulness-for-everyone-podcast-series/